When Breath Becomes Verse

OrangeBooks Publication

1st Floor, Rajhans Arcade, Mall Road, Kohka, Bhilai, Chhattisgarh 490020
Website: **www.orangebooks.in**

First Edition, 2025

ISBN: 978-93-6554-477-0

Price: Rs. 570.00

Printed in India

When Breath Becomes Verse

From a Prayerless Cry to a Faith That Would Never Die

Dr. Prabhakar Shankar

A Poetic Memoir of Loss, Love, and Unspoken Strength

OrangeBooks Publication
www.orangebooks.in

About The Book

When Breath Becomes Verse

A soul's journey from shattered silence to sacred strength.

When Breath Becomes Verse is not just a book.

It's a heartbeat. A battle cry. A resurrection in rhyme.

This unforgettable poetic memoir, penned by Dr. Prabhakar Shankar, chronicles the courageous rise of a man shaped by life's silent storms and sustained by unshaken hope. In the shadows of struggle that tested his spirit, he chose not to break, but to breathe with purpose. He didn't fight with fury, but with unshakable faith. He didn't cry out in pain; he turned his story into power, and his breath into verse.

Told in two soul-stirring parts titled The Story I Never Told and A Lifetime Carved in Writings, this book is not just a collection of poems but a resurrection in rhythm. It transforms pain into poetry, suffering into sacred testimony, and silence into a song of survival. Every verse carries the weight of a truth once buried in silence. Every page bears a scar that chose not just to heal but to shine. This is not merely a story of survival; it is a testament to the human spirit's power to rise, to rebuild, and to rewrite pain into purpose.

From the unseen wounds of childhood to the ache of love that vanished too soon, and from the quiet fire of spiritual awakening to the strength it takes to rise after rejection, *When Breath Becomes Verse* is not just brutally honest; it is beautifully human. It speaks in the voice of those who were never heard, those who were almost broken, and those who survived by becoming something greater.

It is written for the ones who cried alone behind closed doors, for those whose love was left to die, for the warriors who carried battles the world never saw, and for those who rose not because they were ready, but because life left them no other choice.

This book is not just a mirror. It is a hand on your shoulder, a whisper to your soul, and a reminder that even shattered hearts can still arise to paint the world with the loudest purpose.

This is not poetry for performance. This is poetry born in the dark, for the nights that broke in silence. It was carved in shadows, forged through suffering, and carried by breaths that refused to break. These are not just lines on a page; they are echoes of pain, transformed into power.

When Breath Becomes Verse is a literary triumph, a bestselling voice of resilience, a hymn for the broken-hearted, and a timeless companion through the darkest nights where pain still breathes and every word transforms that pain into light.

Preface

There are stories we shout to the world.
And there are stories that live beneath our skin,
aching to be heard,
but too painful to speak.

This is one of those stories.
The one I never told.

Not because I was ashamed.
but because I was still surviving it.

I was born into struggle.
Raised in the shadows of violence, silence, poverty, and broken dreams.
I've tasted blood before I tasted love.
I've been touched in ways a child should never be.
I've seen my father beaten. I've watched my mother bleed.
I've heard the laughter of those who said I wouldn't make it.
And I've cried alone, too many nights to count.

But this isn't a story about sadness.

This is a story about rising anyway.

Through these pages, you will meet the child who limped through school.

The teenager who failed exams and was told he was dumb.

The man who asked God for biryani just to know He was real.

The lover who loved deeply but wasn't accepted.

The fighter who built a life after being broken over and over again.

This book is not decorated with fantasy.

It is not filtered for comfort.

It is raw. It is painful. It is poetry made of real wounds.

But if you're holding this, then maybe, just maybe, you need to be reminded:

You are not alone in your mess.

You are not weak because you feel deeply.

You are not lost because you're still healing.

I wrote this book to give voice to my silence.

But maybe, just maybe, it will give voice to yours too.

So read slowly. Read honestly.

Read when your hands shake. Read when your heart breaks.

And if you find your own story between these lines,

Don't turn away.

Because healing doesn't start when the pain ends.

It starts when the truth is told.

- Dr. Prabhakar Shankar

Index

Part - 1

The Story I Never Told

"I survived what I couldn't speak. These pages carry the silence, the scars, and the strength it took to keep believing there was more than pain".

Chapter – I Raising

"Where my story began, not in light, but in survival."

Endured in silence, behind a brave face,
my childhood hid in a hollowed space.
A quiet ache time couldn't erase.

Chapter – I: Raising

The Story I Never Told

I was born between broken vows and bleeding prayers,
Where my mother's youth was caged at sixteen years.
She whispered goodbyes with abortion pills,
But I held on tight, refusing to disappear.

Seven months deep, she bled again,
Doctors said, "This child may not remain."
But I was not a shadow meant to fade.
I was born on November's fourth, in pain, unafraid.

No doctor caught me, when I came around,
held by nurses in an empty ward, no one else around.
Where weakness fed me through a stranger's care,
A Muslim mother's milk, a Hindu boy's prayer.

At four, I lost my legs to steel and skin,
They said I might never walk again.
Yet grace stitched my feet, and time stitched my pride,
While my mother did homework I couldn't write.

I was scared of my teacher, her stick and her scream,
Yet behind her anger was a hope unseen.
But long before I knew what trust should mean,
I was touched in silence at just thirteen.

No, younger, first grade, innocence torn,
A scar I wear though never sworn.
Too young to name the ache inside,
So, I locked it deep where secrets hide.

I was considered dumb, lost in shame,
Until a clap in fifth grade called my name.
Then games I won, and books I read,
The fire rose where the silence bled.

I sold groundnuts under the palace sky,
Watched cops beat my father, I couldn't cry.
No classroom taught me how to speak,
But a wrestler's roar lit up the weak.

Eighth grade, I led a room with pride,
Tenth grade, topped the school and wide.
The government cheered, gave me ten grands,
The same boy once lost in life's debris.

Then came twelfth with drugs, wars, and fall,
I failed three subjects and nearly lost it all.
I broke my limbs from a stunt of pain,
Fell from floors, but rose again.

Success taught me less than my fall ever did,
It showed me who I am, and what I hid.
This is the story I never told.
Not of a boy, but a spirit bold.

Chapter – II Falling

"Sometimes, hitting the ground is how you touch the divine."

In the shadows of failure, where hope felt rare, pain rose within me to whisper my prayer.

Chapter – II: Falling

Faith In The Midst Of Failure

I failed in twelfth, they laughed aloud,
My dreams lay buried beneath a cloud.
"He's broken now," everyone had said,
"He won't rise; it's in his head."

My kin once spoke to my mother with scorn so steep,
"Your kids are dumb", and all I did was weep.
Too wounded to fight, too numb to speak,
I held my tears, but that didn't make me weak.

I once believed in nothing much,
No holy words, no healing touch.
I kicked the gods, I cursed the sky,
But falling low taught me to cry.

My leg was crushed, my dreams were dust,
My faith in fate began to rust.
My dad was gone, my mom was hurt,
Alone I sat in pain and dirt.

No friends, no light, no helping hand,
Just silence I could barely stand.
No scripture ever made me whole,
But still, I reached with shattered soul.

A Bible sat, untouched, unknown,
Its pages cold, its message thrown.
Yet pain will teach what pride cannot,
And stillness shows the battles fought.

I read. Then paused. Then read again,
Each verse like medicine for pain.
Minutes passed, then turned to hours,
I felt a pull from higher powers.

I whispered low, half-hope, half-test:
"God, send me biryani, then I'll accept and rest.
If You are real, then let me see,
This one small sign, then I'll believe Thee."

And that same night, no feast declared,
No birthdays lit, no table shared.
A neighbour knocked with food in hand,
With biryani, kebab, just as I prayed and planned.

Tears mixed with every bite I took,
Not just for spice, but what it shook.
It wasn't food, it was a sign,
That even I could touch the divine.

I prayed again, not just for meat,
But for guidance to make my purpose complete.
I asked for someone who could teach,
And a preacher came within reach.

I bargained once with God again,
"Let me in college and end this pain.
Give me a seat of doctorate in your name,
And I will walk Your path and you own my fame."

August bowed and the seat was mine,
September 1st, I crossed the line.
I took baptism, left my shame,
And rose again with a brand-new name.

I was the boy they thought would fall,
But I rose, in spite of all.
My wounds were wide, my heart was sore,
But faith rebuilt what life tore.

Chapter – III Healing

"I didn't walk into healing with grace;
I bled through the dark to find my place."

From college corridors to sacred chime,
I stitched myself back one verse, one breath at a time.

Chapter – III: Healing

I Carried Faith In My Backpack

I went to college with prayers, not plans,
With God in my soul and books in my hands.
No dreams of love, no maps to roam,
Just faith in my pocket and fire to own.

Day one arrived, so simple, so plain,
But nothing in life ever comes without gain.
I met a friend, he was a stranger that day,
Who later became the one who chose to stay.

I won the stage, the crowd, the light,
Mr. Fresher crowned me in bright spotlight.
And in the crowd, with silent grace,
Stood my first love with a glowing face.

I said, "Hello," but she smiled so wide,
"I know your name," she softly replied.
She'd seen me preach, seen me pray,
Seen me keep the world at bay.

I kept to God, I kept to peace,
While others danced, I found release
In scriptures read and whispers made,
In quiet talks and nights, I prayed.

But love, it broke like glass too thin,
And grief began to pour within.
The boy who preached, now torn apart,
Found comfort in a bleeding heart.

And suddenly, friends gathered near,
Now they could feel, now they could hear.
One said, “If I could ever choose,
You’d be the one I’d never lose.”

But I saw her only as a friend,
So, I let that chapter softly end.
Then came another, wild and free,
Who said, “Let’s explore the world and see.”

So, I did. With smiles and strife,
I touched the pulse of college life.
I learned, I laughed, I danced, I fell,
In every scar, a story to tell.

In year three, I found my path,
Not in a party, but in Pharma's math.
In medicines, trials, and therapy streams,
I touched the edge of all my dreams.

Then came COVID, dark and wide,
It shook my world, but I did not hide.
While masks were worn and fear ran high,
I stood for home, I didn't cry.

I worked, I served, I made ends meet,
With duty's call beneath my feet.
Curriculum, chaos, both in hand,
Yet still, I chose to boldly stand.

And when it ended, those six long years,
I left with strength, with hope, with tears.
No longer broken, no longer small.
I rose with fire and I had faced it all.

Chapter - IV
Unfolding

"Growth isn't always tender or kind, it burns through the dark to shape your mind."

I broke through betrayal, let go of love, and watched my dreams fall. Yet I stood my ground, rebuilt my name, and rose through it all.

Chapter – IV: Unfolding

Truth Broke Me, Before It Build Me

I stepped into work with a fire so pure,
Logging in early, staying till cure.
While others chased coffee, comfort, and ease,
I bled through my hours, with purpose to please.

But eyes grew bitter, and whispers ran cold,
My sincerity stung, it didn't fit the mold.
Jealousy rose where I gave my all,
And slowly, I watched my passion fall.

I changed my job, I changed my tone,
I learned, unlearned and stood on my own.
While learning life and earning bread,
I searched for love, but faced lies instead.

They wanted money, not my mind,
Love was weightless, worth declined.
So, I made a vow, honest and cold,
"Till I earn my worth, my heart won't unfold."

Then came a ring, a wedding arranged,
But fate had plans it never exchanged.
It shattered quietly, without a sound,
And left me broken, but not unbound.

I paused. I breathed. I quit my race,
Took one month off to find my place.
I stared at mirrors, questioned the pain,
And chose a field where I'd reclaim my name.

I shifted paths with no regret,
And found success where sun had set.
Corporates called. Crowds grew near.
Even married hearts whispered in my ear.

But I said no as I knew my line and stood on my ground.
My growth was quiet, but deeply sound.
I kept my soul from slipping cheap,
And sowed my truth where dreams run deep.

I trained five thousand and gave my flame,
Built my brand, earned my name.
Followers came from far and wide,
But I stood rooted, with no false pride.

Many arrived, and many left,
But through it all, I stayed steadfast.
And just when silence felt like fate.
She came, who was my soulmate.

Chapter – V
Infinity

"True love may not bloom in gentle ways; it sometimes bleeds, yet always stays."

Though torn by time, it stood the test, for some souls were carved in hearts that rest.

Chapter – V: Infinity

Love That Time Couldn't Undo

I met her once and time stood still,
A whisper turned into a will.
From day one, her soul met mine,
Like stars had waited for that sign.

We didn't plan it, didn't force,
Love just flowed its sacred course.
I fell for her in every way,
In words unspoken, in what we'd say.

I met her father, with hope in hand,
But life had drawn a harsher plan.
They said no and they closed the door,
Yet love in us began to roar.

We cried, we fought, we lost our grace,
We mourned on a gift that time can't replace.
So many breakups, storms and rain,
But every time, we loved again.

She held my secrets, dark and deep,
Where silence cuts, and shadows weep.
Still, she stayed, through every wrong,
Still, I loved her all along.

She showed me love like none before,
A kind that heals, not keeps a score.
I loved her back with all I could,
In ways no other ever would.

She chose my soul, though scars were seen,
But her home denied what love could mean.
I said yes, though mine said no,
But hearts don't follow what families know.

Two years passed like winds that burn,
I rose with time, with each return.
Earned in lakhs, stood tall and proud,
Yet faced a layoff in the crowd.

Still here I am not crushed, not gone,
Still singing hope, still holding on.
Still choosing her through rise and fall,
Still believing love will outshine all.

One day her father will see my heart,
One day my kin won't keep us apart.
Till then, we walk not free, not fast,
But hand in hand, in destiny that would ever last.

And when they ask if love is true,
I'll point to the pain we both walked through.
Because real love doesn't fade,
It fights, forgives, and learns to stay.

Part - 2

A Lifetime Carved In Writings

"Scars that learned to speak in verse, where my silence bled into ink, and every verse became a wound that learned to sing".

Chapter – I
The Moment of Childhood

"A Time When Wounds Had No Names"

Before pain had a voice and sorrow found its name,
childhood bloomed in silence, where every wound felt
like flame.

Chapter – 1: The Moment of Childhood

The Birth Of The Redeemer

I was born where coins were few,
On slum dust and morning dew.
A platform merchant's child with dreams to keep,
In huts that hummed the songs of sleep.

My father came like fleeting wind,
A man too lost, too rarely pinned.
Some nights he stayed, most nights he strayed,
And left behind the price we paid.

My mother bore the world on skin,
With broken bangles tucked within.
She cooked on flames of unpaid dues,
And wiped our tears with worn-out shoes.

Some days we dined, some days we prayed,
Some nights the hunger never swayed.
But even when the light grew dim,
I held the dark and learned to swim.

I was the fire the streets would see,
Too wild for walls, too bold to flee.
"Take him," they said, "to temple's gate,
Pierce his ears, before it's too late."

I laughed and said, "Do what you will,
But I won't cry, I will sit still."
The needle stung, the crowd stood dumb,
But not a single tear would come.

The priest, amazed at what I proved,
Reached for a gift that gently moved.
A yellow fruit, so soft and so sweet.
A banana for the child who wouldn't retreat.

But deeper still, my battles ran,
Far from the eyes of god or man.
A kinder surgery stole my days,
Left me behind in quiet haze.

I missed the chalk, the songs, the bell,
Alone with wounds I couldn't tell.
And once I asked, with trembling tone,
"Why did you birth me to break my bone?"

My mother cried but didn't break,
She held me close for healing's sake.
"You were not born for easy roads,
But to carry grace through heavy loads."

When pain began to pull away,
I limped through night but faced the day.
My heart had cracks, but not defeat.
For even fire must earn its flame through feeling the heat.

I joined the school, I passed the test,
With trembling hands and silent rest.
My childhood wasn't sweet or kind,
But it carved a will you'll rarely find.

Not born of silk or silver spoon,
But danced beneath a shattered moon.
And though the world saw just a boy,
I was a storm disguised as joy.

Chapter – II
The Sincere Scholar

"Books became my shelter and grace,
not for the race, but to find my place."

In the storm of silence, books became my shelter, and in the presence of loneliness, words were my mentor

Chapter – II: The Sincere Scholar

The Clap That Changed My Life

Fresh from the blade, still stitched in skin,
I stepped in school, afraid to begin.
My fingers shook, the pencil slipped,
My name, my words, half-formed, half-ripped.

My mom would help, her hands were mine,
Together we wrote, line by line.
The teacher saw, her brows grew tight,
And pain replaced the morning light.

She hit with wood, not words or grace,
Called me "dumb" right to my face.
The world was loud, I stayed unheard,
A lonely heart without a word.

And darker still, where trust should stay,
A girl beside me stole the day.
She crossed the line, she blurred my ground,
But silence made the loudest sound.

I couldn't scream. I couldn't show.
At six years old, how could they know?
I held that wound, too raw to tell,
A quiet child in private hell.

Somehow I passed, though barely whole,
With dreams half-dead and fear in soul.
I walked through halls, unseen, unknown,
But deep inside, I wasn't alone.

Then fifth grade came, a moment rare,
The class sat frozen, blank with stare.
A story of Buddha, none could say,
But I stood up without delay.

I saw the image, saw his face,
And spoke the tale with childlike grace.
No reading skill, no polished part,
Just courage flowing from my heart.

Then came a clap, one single sound,
That shook my roots beneath the ground.
A simple clap, but loud and wide,
That pulled the lost kid back with pride.

From that one clap, I changed my aim,
No longer chasing marks or fame.
I craved the cheer, I chased the spark,
And lit a fire inside the dark.

By sixth I rose in top ten's roll,
By eighth I wore the leader's role.
By ninth I topped, by tenth I shined,
A schoolboy legend, redefined.

The state itself then knew my name,
Ten thousand rupees marked my flame.
A scholar born from stone and strife,
A living verse, a spark of life.

No blueprints used, no shortcuts made,
I studied truth, not marks or grade.
Each chapter read from start to close,
A mind that bloomed like ironed rose.

I learned not English in a classroom rows,
But through wrestling shows.
To hear him speak, I trained my ear,
Each word a step that crushed my fear.

My pen was sharp, my poems flew,
In school's four walls, my spirit grew.
They called me leader, poet, flame,
And every school still remembers my name.

Chapter – III
The Rebellious Teen

"The fall that taught me to rise"

I broke the rules and walked through fire,
Rose from the ashes, shaped by desire.

Chapter – III: The Rebellious Teen

The Fall That Taught Me To Rise

I passed my tenth with stars in hand,
A name well-known across the land.
They said, "He's made it, bright and bold,"
But no one saw the nights about to unfold.

With fame I stepped in eleventh's gate,
But dreams soon bowed beneath their weight.
Fifty kilometres every day,
To school, to class, to lose my way.

I rose with dawn and slept with pain,
No time to breathe, no room to gain.
My books unread, my body worn,
Inside, a quiet storm was born.

That school was not a holy place,
It held no hope, no light, no grace.
With drugs and gangs and poisoned pride,
I clenched my fists and fought the tide.

One boy misstepped, I struck him back,
And suddenly, I was under attack.
A gang war roared from one small spark,
And school became a world too dark.

I told my mom, "I cannot stay",
Please help me find "another way."
But words fell flat, she couldn't see,
The hell that wrapped itself round me.

I fought with teachers, broke my peace,
And watched my hopeful grades decrease.
Physics, Maths, and Bio were gone,
Only Chemistry held on.

And still, I smiled and bought some sweet,
With failing marks and blistered feet.
I told my mom, "Let's celebrate,"
Even failure had its fate.

The ones who once had looked to me,
Now passed with ease, walked proud and free.
A boy who once had called me foe,
Raised his collar and made his show.

He wore his pride; I bowed my head,
Ashamed of all the tears I shed.
Then Mom compelled, "Go to kin's town,"
But battles there had just begun.

I reached my kin's home not as a guest,
But as a failure, not allowed to rest.
No books, no dreams, just pots and floors,
A prisoner behind unlocked doors.

One day, I tried to touch the sky,
To feel again what it meant to fly.
A stunt, a leap from third to second,
But gravity had its lesson reckoned.

My leg gave way, my body bruised,
Thrown back home, discarded, used.
Even for surgery, I had to plead.
Like I was less than one in need.

I wept and questioned my fate,
My heart was loud, my soul irate.
I trusted none, I bled alone,
But pain carved a deeper tone.

That moment came; I couldn't stand.
I watched respect slip from each hand.
And in that silence, something stirred.
Not a voice, but a whisper heard.

I realized then, through bone and tear,
That power lies in rising here.
That if I walk, I walk alone,
But strength is something self-grown.

The surgery passed, I healed with fire,
A rebel now with new desire.
My teen years broke me, left me torn,
But from that break, a man was born.

They said I was broken, said I was slow,
But they never saw how high I'd go.
For some boys break, and some boys burn,
And some just wait for their time to return.

Chapter - IV
The Divine Seeker

"When silence spoke and heavens heard"

A soul's journey from shattered nights to sacred light.

Chapter – IV: The Divine Seeker

The Journey To Sacred Light

The house was still, the night was deep,
I lay alone, too lost to weep.
No father's voice, no guiding hand,
Just broken dreams and shifting sand.

My mother, too, with wounds to hide,
Lay stitched in silence, pained inside.
The world outside kept turning fast,
But I was trapped within my past.

A rebel heart, a skeptic soul,
I didn't need a higher goal.
But emptiness became my flame,
And in that void, someone came.

Beside my bed, in silent grace,
A Bible rested, out of place.
I felt strange and I was unclear,
Yet something holy lingered near.

I reached and turned a trembling page,
A boy, not saint, not wise, not sage.
Just tired eyes and aching bone,
But when I read, I wasn't alone.

The words were soft, the meaning dim,
Yet peace began to flow from Him.
Each verse I read, I felt a shift,
A soul once sunken now could lift.

Each day I'd read, and something grew,
The text I feared now felt like dew.
In every line, I found a truth of its own.
I admired every verse that was renowned.

I told my pain, I spoke my dreams,
My selfish thoughts, my silent screams.
And as I prayed, the hours flew,
And when I slept, I was healing through divine dew.

No footsteps out, no worldly call,
For eight long months, I faced it all.
Just home and hope, and hospital beds,
While prayers danced above my dreads.

A broken leg, but soul made whole,
For now, I saw my higher role.
I told the Lord, “make me rise’,
Before my ‘enemies eyes.”

I tested faith with hungry eyes,
“If You are real, then send out a biryani as a surprise.”
That very day, as if on cue, biryani came.
And I understood Almighty’s name and fame.

Eighteen years a Hindu child,
Now torn by grace so strange and wild.
How could I start this life anew?
But faith had come, and faith felt true.

Then came the test, the entrance gate,
And I walked through with hands of fate.
Doctorate, my dream made real,
With folded hands and heart to kneel.

Before I packed for college halls,
I heard the final, gentle call.
Baptized not with pride or fear,
But with a soul that now stood clear.

I didn't find God in temple sound,
But in the silence and difficult ground.
I sought a sign. He gave me bread.
And poured His light where I once bled.

No preacher called, no altar flame,
Just hunger, tears, and whispered name.
And now I walk free, but not blind,
For faith first found and showed that God is kind.

And now I walk with faith, not sight,
It held me through my loneliest night.
Grace didn't come with blinding light,
It came in silence, soft and right.

Chapter – V
Soul On Crutches

"The crutch that carried my soul"

I didn't just walk with it. I lived because of it.

Chapter – V: Soul On Crutches

Silence On Borrowed Limbs

I was broken not just in bone,
But in the silence, I walked alone.
The world had left, the noise had died,
And faith was all I had inside.

My twelfth exam loomed fierce and near,
But doubt was loud in every ear.
"He failed before, when whole and strong,
Now crushed and weak, he won't last long."

My own kin scoffed, their voices cold,
"Your son is broken, bruised, and old.
He couldn't pass in brighter days,
Now he will fall in darker ways."

My mother wept but couldn't speak,
She begged for help, her voice so weak.
Even my surgery came with pain,
No comfort there, no cleansing rain.

The needle pierced my very spine,
But still I said, "This fight is mine."
Though even she had lost her flame,
I whispered soft, "God knows my name."

No hands to hold me when I cried,
No friend to kneel there by my side.
Just metal arms beneath my grip,
And prayers born from a trembling lip.

A walker first, so slow, so loud,
A crutch that made me feel unbowed.
Not for a day, or week, or part,
That crutch became a limb, a heart.

It watched me weep when I was numb,
It saw me break, it made me come
Back from the dead, back from the ache,
Each silent step, a quake I'd make.

From bed to bath, from dawn to dusk,
It bore the weight when legs would rest.
More than steel, it bore my soul,
A silent friend that made me whole.

It didn't judge, it didn't speak,
But in its silence, I found meek.
And every tear that found the floor,
Was caught by grace, and nothing more.

They said, "Let us help you climb,"
But I refused, this pain is mine.
My exam was high on terrace floor,
No lift, no help, just stairs and war.

So I climbed slow, with breath and brace,
While shame tried crawling up my face.
They saw a boy with bent-down knees,
But I was flying on worn-out wings.

I passed that test with burning limb,
God was one, who made me climb.
Through every fall, He heard my call,
And crutches stayed to see it all.

It wasn't just a stick of steel,
It knew the things that God could feel.
My faith, my grief, my silent fight,
It walked me out of endless night.

And when they ask me what I need,
I point not up, I point beneath.
For that old crutch, that metal grace,
Still lives in heart, in soul, in place.

"He'll never run," they used to say,
But I had touched the edge of day.
My steps were cracked, my rhythm torn,
Yet in that limp, new strength was born.

That crutch wasn't aid, it was a vow,
To walk again, despite the "how."
It didn't hold just bone and skin,
It held the storm I kept within.

And when my name is lit in fire,
Know this, I limped, but climbed up higher.
For I was never just a boy in abstain,
I was a soul on crutches, walking through pain.

Chapter – VI
The First Step After The Fall

"Walked again, not fast but bold."

"I rose not with speed, but with grace, each step a triumph time couldn't erase."

Chapter – VI: The First Step After The Fall

I Didn't Just Rise, But Answered All

Eight months I lay, both torn and still,
Battling not just bone, but broken will.
Not just my leg that couldn't bend,
But a soul that begged for pain to end.

No sun had touched my crumpled skin,
No door had dared to let me in.
I lay not just with shattered bone,
But with a heart carved out of stone.

Each day I stared at ceiling white,
A battlefield beneath the light.
No guests, no cheers, no flowers sent,
Just breath and grief, and limbs half-bent.

They think that healing comes with rest,
But no one saw the hidden test.
To lie in bed while time walked past,
And wonder if this pain would last.

I told my mom with trembling voice,
"I won't step out till I earn my choice."
A doctorate seat, my vow, my fight,
My only spark through darkest night.

They stared at me, some with a grin,
"Look at him, can't walk, but thinks he'll win."
Even my kin, they laughed behind,
Mocked my limp with hollow mind.

No left foot touched the earth below,
No temple ground, no wind, no snow.
For eight whole months, I stayed inside,
A place where God chose to unhide.

But slowly, softly, spark found skin,
And light returned from deep within.
One quiet day, no crowd, no cry,
I dropped my crutches, dared to try.

My foot, my left, once numb, once curled,
Descended soft into the world.
And when it kissed the dusty floor,
The dead in me began to roar.

It wasn't speed, it wasn't pride,
But fire that I could no longer hide.
I walked again, not fast, not loud,
But bold enough to shame the crowd.

And when I rose with college seat,
The same mouths silenced in defeat.
Those who mocked now bowed their eyes,
Not for my pride, but for their lies.

I didn't walk to prove them wrong,
I walked to where I once belonged.
Not to explore what's out and wide,
But all I held and hurt inside.

For in that bed, in pain's own womb,
The old me died to make me bloom.
Not fast. Not proud. Nor forged in gold.
But walking now, not fast, but bold.

My leg was broken, but my spine was steel,
Each step I took began to heal.
They saw a limp. I saw my fight,
To rise from endless, sleepless night.

I didn't race. I didn't run,
But I outwalked what weighed a ton.
And now when asked what pain can mold,
I say, "I walk, not fast, but bold."

Chapter – VII
The Hidden Calling

"I heard his voice in my dreams."

When heaven whispered my name, I was adored in blue,
a purpose born true.

Chapter – VII: The Hidden Calling

His Voice In My Dream

I walked a road of grace unknown,
Led by light I hadn't sown.
The path was soft, the sky was wide,
And faith began to walk beside.

I didn't know what lay ahead,
But still, I followed where He led.
And slowly, through the veil and mist,
I felt a truth I once dismissed.

I told my mom, "Come join me too,
Let's walk where hearts are born anew."
She saw my peace, she saw me shine,
And stepped into that sacred line.

But one still night, when all was still,
God called me higher, called me real.
A dream, but more than sleep could show,
A world the waking never know.

He stood before me, bathed in light,
More dazzling than the stars at night.
His robe was white with checks in gold,
A beauty words have never told.

I wore a shirt of quiet blue,
But something loud was breaking through.
Not stitched in cloth, but soul and flame,
The night the Lord first spoke my name.

Not in a crowd, not in a song,
But in a dream where I belong.
He called me His, He called me true,
And purpose woke inside that blue.

And there He stood, so wide and tall,
More bright than stars that dare to fall.
His face outshone the burning sun,
Yet looked at me, the broken one.

His hair, like sun on rivers spun,
His face outshone a million suns.
And there I knelt, my pride undone,
Before the feet of Heaven's Son.

His feet were pierced, worn, and bare,
Yet held more love than I could bear.
I touch his feet and kissed them deep and low,
And felt the weight of love I would ever know.

"I'm nothing, Lord," was all I said.
He raised me up and smiled instead.
"You've walked through storms, you've paid your price.
You are My flame, My sacrifice."

He called me martyr, called me friend,
He told me, "This is not the end.
You've earned this not through crown or fame,
But in the dark, you spoke My name."

It burned within and carved my soul,
And filled the cracks that once were whole.
From that day on, my life had flame,
And I Knew, I would never walk the same.

I saw the angels in my dreams,
Their wings like fire, their voices beams.
They took me to the mountains gold,
Where heaven's light was pure and cold.

The snow was light, but warm and wise,
And praise poured down from flawless skies.
They called me blessed, they called me known,
And claimed my spirit as their own.

I told the saints, "I saw His face."
They said, "We've never felt that grace."
And I, confused, just bowed my head,
Not knowing what the Lord had said.

But time passed by, and I could see,
His hidden hand was shaping me.
Visions came, and peace grew deep,
Even in storms, I found my sleep.

He whispered once, "The world shall change,"
And time soon turned to something strange.
Yet through the storm, I stood and knew,
My purpose bloomed, my spirit grew.

The world was drowning in disease,
Yet I walked through it all with ease.
I said, "Lord, why do I still stand?"
He whispered softly, "By My hand."

I found my voice in dreams so bright,
And walked by faith, not by sight.
For some are called in temple hall,
But I was chosen through night's call.

And now I rise, with soul aware,
That Heaven hears my praise and prayer.
Not for the world or stage or song,
But for a God who makes me strong.

Chapter – VIII
Sacred Collapse

"A heartbreak not from Heaven, but from earth."

The prayers fell silent, the skies stayed dim. It wasn't God who broke me, it was them.

Chapter – VIII: Sacred Collapse

A Heartbreak From Earth

I believed in God with all my soul,
More than silver, more than gold.
I prayed for truth, I craved His voice,
And when He called, I made my choice.

I followed preachers, heard their word,
Each sermon like a flame I heard.
I knelt in pews, I raised my hand,
I walked where I was told to stand.

Their verses rang like sacred song,
And there I knew where I belong.
I gave my heart, I gave my time,
Believed in every word and rhyme.

I gave my coin to build His home,
A sacred space of stone and dome.
They said, "This house is God's own land,"
And so I gave with open hand.

But cracks appeared behind the stage,
Not in the walls, but in their rage.
For truth once whispered, loud and plain,
Now bowed to fame and offered gain.

I watched the flock forget His face,
And claimed the altar as their space.
Where boys chased girls, and hearts played game,
And no one prayed, just thirst for name.

I saw the people walk in pride,
With empty souls, and hands untried.
They came not for the voice above,
But just to find convenience, love.

A preacher said, "Build up the hall."
Another asked, "Did God say that at all?"
And suddenly, the veil was torn,
And every truth felt crushed and worn.

I wept not for my God above,
But for the lies dressed up as love.
I wasn't hurt by Heaven's grace,
But by the masks that wore His face.

I felt betrayed, not by His hand,
But by the ones who took His stand.
They preached of light, but loved their fame,
And used the cross to build their name.

So, I let go, not of my faith,
But of their words laced thick with wraith.
No longer blind, I walked away,
But still I knelt. I still would pray.

I stopped the shows, the chants, the crowd,
The staged-up lights, the music loud.
And found Him not in fame or dome,
But in the silence of my home.

I still would sit. I still would speak.
To the same God I once did seek.
But now alone, no stage, no name,
Just me and Him, and that's the flame.

They built Him temples, gold and wide,
But lost the God they claimed inside.
And though their altars turned to dust,
I kept my faith, I kept my trust.

For Heaven doesn’t trade its light
To men who preach with selfish might.
And even when their kingdoms fall,
God kneels with me, beyond it all.

Chapter – IX
Heart's First Whisper

"A love too true for the time to hold."

It came like dawn, with a glow so rare, yet vanished like mist in morning air.

Chapter – IX: Heart's First Whisper

The One-Month Forever

They say that love begins in school days,
In classroom glances and reckless plays.
Mine began with ink and grace,
In pages where her hand left trace.

She helped me write, she helped me heal,
And what I asked, she'd give with zeal.
I asked for one page note,
She gave me forty pages of love note.

Another time, so young, so shy,
A girl had asked with lowered eye.
A letter scrawled, a folded heart,
But I said no, and stepped apart.

Then college came with brighter days,
I never knew life held such ways.
"Mr. Fresher!", they called me aloud,
And there she stood, beyond the crowd.

I said, "Hello," she smiled so wide,
"I know your name," her voice replied.
She'd seen me pray, she'd seen me preach,
Before I thought, she chose to reach.

She was my senior, kind and wise,
She gave me books with warmth her eyes.
She spoke when I had lost my voice,
And stayed when staying wasn't choice.

Her eyes met mine, a quiet spark,
Like sunrise cutting through the dark.
She smiled as if she'd always known,
And in that glance, she said you're mine and mine alone.

She called me out when I fell still,
She brought me food, she bore my will.
And there she was, no games, no lies, only grace,
Just her love met me face to face.

She prayed together for every need,
And loved with reverence, not with greed.
We spoke in verses, not in lust,
With every glance, a sacred trust.

But age stood tall and states grew wide,
And bloodline rules tore us aside.
I was younger, and they said "no",
They couldn't see what hearts can know.

Her brother forced her to let go,
Behind a door, her tears would flow.
She wept in silence, held her breath,
While I just stared and prayed for death.

I cried alone within my room,
My mother sensed the silent gloom.
She never asked the reason why,
Some griefs are taught to never cry.

Our love, it lived for just a moon,
A one-month tale that died too soon.
No touch, no sin, no broken vow,
Just purest love the world won't allow.

Her books I read, still smelled like peace,
Like jasmine folded in the crease.
I was her first, she was my flame,
But fate, not fault, had played the game.

She loved me deep, she loved me fast,
And swore that I would be her last.
We parted not with hate or blame,
Just silent ache we couldn't tame.

Not every love is meant to stay,
Some bloom, then softly fade away.
But this one lives, both clean and true,
In every class, in every blue.

We never kissed, we never lied,
But still it hurt when we both cried.
And though the world forgot her name,
She was my spark, my quiet flame.

Chapter – X
Combat Of Soul

"The battle that brought me back."

I stepped in with pain. I walked out with peace. I wasn't chasing belts. I was chasing breath.

Chapter – X: Combat Of Soul

My War Never With The World

After love had left me torn,
Every dream felt stillborn,
I lay in bed with the weight of days,
As breathless dreams dissolved in haze.

My leg had healed, but not my mind,
So many scars I couldn't find.
No joy, no touch, no breath felt right,
Just memories lost in endless night.

I lay in shadows, drowning slow,
With no place left for light to go.
Then in the dark, a whisper stirred,
A childhood flame I had not heard.

Martial arts, a name once mine,
Now called me back, a sacred sign.
Not to fight, not to display,
But just to keep the pain at bay.

Not for medals, not for cheers,
But for the silence in my ears.
To fight the noise inside my chest,
At last, to find a sweet place to rest.

I rose again, not fast, not grand,
But steady with a shaking hand.
Each punch I threw, each move I made,
Unwrote the wounds I never said.

Weapons twirled and limbs would fly,
But deeper wars lived in my eye.
I wasn't there to beat a name,
But to burn the shame that hid in flame.

And as I moved, my soul grew still,
I found in combat, a greater will.
My breath aligned, my spirit bent,
And through the form, my heart was sent.

I earned the black, I earned the grace,
With tears still shining on my face.
The belt wasn't a prize to wear,
It was the proof that I was there.

I stood for state, I stood for pride,
But deeper still, I stood inside.
The boy once mocked for broken legs,
Now danced with swords on shattered pegs.

And more than fights or shining steel,
I taught young hearts how wounds can heal.
I passed the art, I gave it voice,
To show that strength is still a choice.

No longer just a fractured frame,
But now a master of the flame.
And though I've bled from soul to skin,
I've found the calm that lives within.

They said I'd never walk again,
Now I move like the roaring wind.
I didn't train to conquer land,
I fought to simply understand.

Not every strike is thrown for show,
Some break the parts we never show.
And though I fought through loss and role,
The hardest war was in my soul.

I wasn't built in gyms or fame,
But in the dark, through silent flame.
They broke my heart, they broke my limb,
But never guessed how high I'd climb.

I didn't fight to wound or kill,
I fought to give my soul its will.
The world saw belts and cheered my name,
But only I knew why I came.

Chapter – XI
Warrior's Crown

"I bled to find peace, not applause."

I stepped in with pain, not seeking fame, but rose with fortune or name.

Chapter – XI: Warrior's Crown

Crowning Moment Of Inner Mastery

I did not train in polished halls,
No mats to break the aching falls.
The days were long, the nights would freeze,
But sweat became my only peace.

No punching bags, no cheering crowd,
Just broken bricks and cries aloud.
My knuckles bled on walls of home,
Yet every blow, my soul felt the bloom.

The floor was cracked, the roof was bare,
But discipline was in the air.
My fist met stone, again, again,
Till when I outgrew the name of pain.

I didn't dream of gold or praise,
I didn't fight for name or place.
The medals came, but weren't my goal,
I fought to resurrect my soul.

My arms grew strong, my breath turned steel,
Yet silence was all I would feel.
For what's a belt if you're not whole?
The hardest fight's to wield the soul.

Yes, I was called by state and pride,
To stand for flag with flames inside.
But deeper than the flag or fame,
Was how I stitched my soul and name.

They saw my stance, my battle cry,
But never saw the nights that went dry.
No one knew the wars I braved,
The self I lost, the self I saved.

I bowed before no worldly king,
My crown was carved from suffering.
No trophies gave me what I sought,
But peace, that pain and practice bought.

Non-violence marked my truest fight,
To lift my hands, devoid of spite.
To cage the storm that burned within,
And wear restraint as discipline.

I wielded weapons sharp and cold,
But never let them harm or hold.
For what I pierced was not the skin,
But lies I carried deep within.

They cheered my name across the seas,
Their banners waved in victory's breeze.
But I bowed low with humble face,
For I had found a higher place.

I did not want the world to kneel,
I only longed for wounds to heal.
And life, in silence, placed a crown,
Upon the head once cast down.

Each wound I bear, a whispered vow,
To never kneel, no matter how.
I bled in rooms where no one came,
And turned that pain into my flame.

They saw the medals, not the nights
I screamed alone in shadowed fights.
I wasn't shaped by hands or cheers,
But by surviving silent years.

No stage could hold the war I faced,
No trophy knows the nights I braced.
I walked through hell with burning feet,
And stitched my soul through each defeat.

Chapter - XII
Souls Of Other Side

"The hug I never knew I needed."

A stranger's arms spoke what words couldn't say,
borders dissolved, and the ache slipped away.

Chapter – XII: Souls Of Other Side

In That Warmth, A Wound Was Healed

I thought I knew this world so well,
The lands, the names, the flags that swell.
But fate had ways I couldn't chart,
It brought me souls that healed my heart.

From distant lands with foreign skies,
They smiled at me with warmer eyes.
No blood, no bond, no common name,
And yet, they loved me just the same.

She wasn't born on native sand,
She spoke with grace, her voice was grand.
We barely met, just classmates then,
But something soft began again.

She needed help in a test, a fight,
I stayed with her through day and night.
And when it passed, she turned around,
And gave a hug without a sound.

No one had held me quite that way,
Not friends, not kin, not yesterday.
Her arms were light, but full and deep,
Like all the love I couldn't keep.

It wasn't love, it wasn't lust,
It bloomed in silence, pure and just.
A thank you carved in skin and bone,
That made me feel less lost, less alone.

And in that hug, the world stood still,
A boy once broken bent to heal.
A woman's care, not claimed or owed,
But given sweetly, just bestowed.

Then came a brother from afar,
Who read my fate like guiding star.
He saw the things I'd tried to hide,
And said, "Your fire burns inside."

He didn’t preach, he didn’t boast,
But filled my cup when I needed most.
His faith in me was like a song,
That made me feel I still belonged.

Their hands were strange, their tongues unknown,
Yet in their eyes, a warmth was shown.
They loved beyond the lines of land,
A touch only I can understand.

I used to think my world was small,
Just borders, walls, and narrow hall.
But they, like winds from foreign tide,
Showed me the souls on the other side.

Not every hug must end in vow,
Some moments just are here and now.
And though our paths may drift or part,
They stitched new seams into my heart.

So, if you ask what changed my view,
It wasn't books or skies of blue.
It was a hug, a friend, a flame,
From lands that never knew my name.

Chapter – XIII
Night That Refused To End

"For the fire within refused to end."

The night was long, the light grew thin, but I held the fire deep within.

Chapter – XIII: Night That Refused To End

In Darkness, I Rose Without A Name

The books were open, so was I the night
With sleepless eyes, the pen was held tight,
The syllabus new, the pressure wide,
But still I burned with passion inside.

This wasn't fate, this wasn't guess,
I chose this path in full awareness.
Each word I read was like a vow,
To keep my dream, no matter how.

But something stirred I couldn't name,
A creeping heat, a silent flame.
My skin grew hot, my body weak,
But I still had a test to seek.

"Maybe it's just the sleepless nights,"
I told myself between the fights.
My mom had gone, I stayed alone,
In shadows deeper than I'd known.

A chill ran deep into my bone,
A pain that whispered, "You're on your own."
I called her late, my breath was thin,
"I don't feel right, can you come in?"

She came at once, no questions loud,
Just worry cloaked like morning cloud.
That night was long, it had no end,
A blur of pain I couldn't defend.

My body raged, but mind stood tall,
"I must still write, I can't fall."
The world may pause, but I must grow,
For dreams can't be outshined by fever's glow.

Red-faced, trembling, cold in skin,
But still I held the fire within.
I walked to class like nothing tore,
And wrote my pain in paper's core.

They saw the red and called it stress,
But only I knew the burning mess.
I finished lines and left the hall,
Then let the weight to fall.

I hit the bed like waves to shore,
And slept a sleep I can't ignore.
But when I woke, the truth had bled,
The word they said was "Dengue," dread.

A name, a storm, a shattered frame,
Illness suddenly came with a name.
It changed my course, it stung my flame,
And nothing after felt the same.

But still I stood, still told the sky,
"I've seen worse things, I will not die."
I laughed a little, tried to cope,
But never knew I'd miss that hope.

For even fire must find its ash,
Even strong souls sometimes crash.
And though I walked through that exam,
A part of me forgot who I am.

The night that bled into my bones,
Still haunts me when I'm all alone.
But still I smile and say, "I went."
For even hell won't make me bent.

So if you ask what forged my soul,
It wasn't dreams, it was control.
And if you ask why I still bend,
It's because I lived that night that wouldn't end.

Chapter – XIV
Cradled By The End

"When death came close and all seemed gone, a spark within still carried me on."

I stared at the edge with breath grown thin, but chose to fight the war within.

Chapter – XIV: Cradled By The End

Held By The End, But Chose To Ascend

It came one night, no grand alarm,
No thunderclap, no omen charm.
Just fevered chills and aching skin,
A war I never knew would begin.

I'd faced the break of bones before,
Felt heartbreak pound my inner core.
But nothing gripped me quite like this,
A burning scream, a venomous kiss.

Dengue, the name that turned me red,
My body pulsed, my blood had fled.
Each breath I took, a mountain climb,
Each minute felt like borrowed time.

My gums would bleed, my stomach swell,
I walked the borders close to hell.
My voice was faint, my hope grew thin,
But still, I wouldn't let death in.

I saw two white-coat novices by my bed,
Their eyes held neither fear nor dread
And one of them said, "He may not rise,"
And death looked deep into my eyes.

But I said no. Not now. Not yet.
My soul was loud, my will was set.
I didn't scream. I didn't cry.
I simply whispered, "I can't die."

I won't let pain define my end,
I won't forget how blood can mend.
I won't let trauma steal my name,
I'll rise again, through ash and flame.

For I have loved and I have lost,
And still I choose to bear the cost.
I've fought through fire, flood, and fall,
And now I know the worth of all.

They laid me down in sterile light,
As doctors whispered through the night.
One shook his head, then said, "We've tried,
You take him elsewhere and sighed.

My mother cried, her knees hit ground,
"Please save my son," was all she found.
She begged beneath a doctor's feet,
While I lay crushed in fever's heat.

My mother wept and cursed the skies,
She forsook her God with tear-filled eyes.
But I said, "Don't grieve, don't fall apart,
Even in death, I'll have His heart."

My platelets dropped, below six grand,
The numbers slipped through slipping hands.
"Shift to ICU," the nurse had said,
"This night may hold him, or his end."

My skin grew blotched, my breath turned slow,
And death stood near, as if to show,
That life's not kept by strength or pride,
But those who kneel and fight beside.

Then came the call, the blood was low,
But friends and strangers made it flow.
Thirteen souls, both known and not,
Arrived with blood, a gift they brought.

A girl I hugged, a boy I knew,
All came to give a part of you.
And in that bag, that crimson stream,
Was love that stitched my shattered dream.

The platelets surged, my body stirred,
And hope returned like newborn word.
I healed, though slow, from edge and crack,
From hell itself, I staggered back.

And through it all, one truth rang clear,
We don't know life, until death's near.
We don't feel breath until it's faint,
We don't touch God till hearts grow saint.

In the midst of exam, I almost lost my breath.
I walked through hands held close by death.
And when they ask, "How did you live?"
I say, 'By grace, Almighty chose to give.'

I give my pain, my truth, my fight,
To every soul who fears the night.
To every heart that's lamenting within,
Just hold your breath, and say, "I'll win."

Chapter - XV
Twilight Of Hope

"Some bonds are carved in blood not by birth, but by kindness and beyond it."

Some bonds are born not from womb, but from wounds, sealed in silence, and shaped by sorrow.

Chapter – XV: Twilight Of Hope

Some Ties Aren't Chosen

He came from lands beyond my own,
With different roots, a different tone.
Yet in his eyes, a light ran deep,
A bond that time was meant to keep.

While others mocked or turned their face,
I offered help, I gave them space.
In books and tasks, I held their hand,
They stood, because I helped them stand.

And then came he, with heart so wide,
He walked not near, but walked beside.
Not just a friend, but something more,
A brother that my soul adore.

He gave not words, but gave his vein,
He shared his blood to ease my pain.
He saw me weak, my spirit dry,
And brought me juice, he heard my cry.

He placed it down with gentle grace,
No pride, no fuss, just calm embrace.
And in that sip, I tasted proof,
That love can heal beneath the roof.

He gifted me a scarf of care,
To guard the storms my soul would bear.
A cap he placed upon my head,
And softly, smiling, this he said.

“This cap, for you, a leader’s sign,
The scarf, to keep your soul in line.
You give with heart, you teach with light,
So wear them both and walk with might.”

No gold, no fame, no grand award,
But these two gifts were love’s reward.
For in his acts so small, so true,
He showed me skies I never knew.

We never called it “brotherhood,”
But every silence said we could.
He saw me when the rest looked past,
And held me when my hope was last.

But time, it moved with silent feet,
And life cut short what felt complete.
He left the course, he slipped away,
No message left, no word to say.

Now every scarf I wrap at dawn,
Reminds me of the friend who's gone.
Each time I touch that gifted cap,
I feel his soul within my lap.

I search for signs, I watch the sky,
I wonder if he too asks why.
If fate still writes him in my page,
Or left him lost in time and age.

He gave his blood, but more than that,
He gave me hope where none once sat.
A foreign friend? No, much more true,
A brother dressed in different hue.

And if these lines ever find his way,
I hope he reads and that's all I pray.
You mattered then. You matter still.
And I will wait, I always will.

Chapter - XVI
The Start Of Forever

"When everyone left and silence grew loud, the only soul stayed among the crowd."

In a world that moved and drifted away, one heart held on, and chose to stay.

Chapter – XVI: The Start Of Forever

The Friend Who Stayed

I met him once, in hallway light,
No stars, no sparks, no fate in sight.
But life, in silence, took its pen,
And wrote our bond in ink and then.

We laughed, we fought, we shared the air,
In college parks, we lingered there.
Where others courted, hand in hand,
We sat and spoke, no grander plan.

No promises, no contracts signed,
Just hours lost and souls aligned.
When I fell sick, when strength would fade,
He knelt beside the mess I made.

When I could not write, he held my pen,
He wrote my words again, again.
When teachers frowned and closed the door,
He stood as gate and gave me more.

He forged the name upon my page,
And fought my wars despite the rage.
He crossed the town, he bore the cost,
He made me win when all felt lost.

And when my bones were cut once more,
He waited there outside that door.
Not with flowers, not with flair,
But with his silence, support and care.

They say a friend is tried by need,
But he was root, and I was seed.
I stood for him through nights unclear,
When grief had dried his every tear.

His father died, his world turned black,
But I held him and pulled him back.
I told him, "Study, chase the light,"
But he was lost in other fight.

Yet still I stayed, no words to blame,
Just walked with him through silent shame.
And now we stand through time and tide
No matter what the world decide.

For friendship isn't built on ease,
But on the storms we didn't freeze.
Not born of blood, but soul and vow,
We stand together then and now.

The world may change, the pages turn,
But fire like this will always burn.
Our laughs, our scars, our midnight talks,
Still echo in those college walks.

So, if you ask what made me whole,
It wasn't love, or fame, or goal.
It was a boy with quiet grace,
Who gave me strength, who took my place.

And though no medal bears his name,
He walked with me through fire and flame.
A friend who stayed, when all had gone,
And helped me write my moving dawn.

Chapter - XVII
When Passion Meets Purpose

"It wasn't just science, or books on a shelf, it was the purpose that pulled me back to myself."

It wasn't the knowledge that made me whole, it was the purpose that gently healed my soul.

Chapter – XVII: When Passion Meets Purpose

The Medicine That Healed Me

I came with wounds that time could trace,
With fractured bones and broken grace.
I'd known the sting of soul betrayed,
Where even faith had disobeyed.

But something stirred, a quiet flame,
Not for the prize, nor worldly name.
A shift began inside my chest,
A calling found within unrest.

At Swat I stood, not saint, not sage,
But eyes now burning off the page.
I slept with books beside my bed,
Their silent words danced in my head.

No longer just to pass or score
But to understand the body's core.
Each cell, each nerve, each aching cry,
I studied not the "how" but "why."

Medicine was never just a book to read,
But a heartbeat answered when hearts bleed.
Not facts to memorize or charts to write,
But healing souls through human light.

I touched each term with reverence raw,
As if God's breath spoke through each law.
The human form, both fierce and warm,
Became a refuge for my storm.

I never chased the praise or prize,
But truth that lit the darkest skies.
And in the quiet, silent race,
I found my fire; I found my place.

I taught my peers, I held their hand,
I built them where they tried to stand.
Without a thought, I took that lead,
Not for applause, but out of need.

And in those rooms of sterile white,
I found my fire, I found my rite.
From martial strikes to silent prayer,
Healing rose, beyond the care.

It wasn't fate that led me here,
It wasn't luck or fleeting cheer.
It was the pain, the trials, the knife,
That made this path my pulse, my life.

This wasn't just a course I chose,
It was the salve to all my throes.
The medicine that stitched my soul,
And made my fractured spirit whole.

Not everyone can drink this tea,
For some it's just a damn degree.
But I bled to earn this right,
To see the body, soul, and light.

And now I walk with scalpel grace,
No longer running any race.
This isn't just my dream come true,
It's who I am, through and through.

From broken bones to hearts once numb,
My passion called, and I have come.
I didn't choose this just to strive,
This medicine made me alive.

Chapter - XVIII
Blooming Life

"From silence to smiles, from pain to presence."

From the soil of silence and grief so deep, I found a self I swore to keep.

Chapter – XVIII: Blooming Life

From Pain I Rose, Into A Soul I Chose

I once walked halls in silent gloom,
A shadow within my study room.
Where dreams felt faint and words were few,
And every face just flickered through.

But time, it whispered soft and slow,
"Come out, dear soul, it's time to grow."
So, I obeyed, with trembling grace,
And wore a smile upon my face.

I laughed when laughter brushed my skin,
Let friendship slowly pull me in.
The boy once roaming streets alone,
Now found some hands to call his own.

A chair was saved, a name was called,
In quiet ways, I felt enthralled.
To eat, to speak, to joke, to roam,
I found a world and called it home.

The walls I built began to crack,
And joy, once distant, trickled back.
A seminar, a crowded street,
New places where my soul could meet.

Butterflies danced in my chest,
As life awoke from years of rest.
The boy who feared the world outside,
Now laughed aloud, no need to hide.

I wasn't chasing lofty dreams,
Just living life in humble streams.
Not purpose now, but pulse and play,
To taste the beauty of each day.

Yet somewhere in this bloom and cheer,
A part of me still held the tear.
For joy, so loud, can hum with ache,
When healing hearts begin to break.

Because I knew, beneath it all,
That friendships rise and some may fall.
That even smiles can sometimes sting,
When trust begins unravelling.

But still I bloomed, through fear and fight,
A candle dancing into light.
No longer lost, no longer cold,
I learned to live, and love, and hold.

So if you see me shining now,
Know well the scars I bear below.
For every bloom that tastes of sweet,
Grew from a root wrapped in defeat.

Chapter - XIX
When A Friend Called It Love

"She gave me her heart; I only had silence."

She held my hand like it was fate, but I only saw a friend, I couldn't reciprocate.

Chapter – XIX: When A Friend Called It Love

She Saw Forever, I Saw A Friend

I opened doors and let them in,
Let friendships bloom beneath my skin.
Some stayed within the space I gave,
While others crossed the silent wave.

She came so soft, with steps so near,
Her presence calm, her voice sincere.
She walked beside me, day and night,
And filled my air with gentle light.

To me, she was a loyal friend,
No signs of more, no hearts to mend.
But in her gaze, a different hue,
She saw in me a lover true.

She spoke in hints, in quiet ways,
In borrowed time and stretching days.
Then once, she said, without disguise,
"If I propose, you'll be my prize."

Her words were warm, but I stood still,
For love can't bloom against the will.
I told her softly, not unkind,
"You'll find someone more aligned."

She smiled outside, but cracked inside,
And from that day, I stepped aside.
Her silence screamed what lips denied,
A heartbreak she could never hide.

She nodded yes, but meant a no,
And let her inner sorrow grow.
I knew I wasn't hers to hold,
And truth, though sharp, must still be told.

But love, when pure, is like a stream,
That crashes quietly through a dream.
A stone we throw to shield our shore,
Still sends its ripples evermore.

I never meant to dim her light,
Or take her stars away at night.
But hearts don't match by force or fate,
And love won't grow from second-rate.

So, I moved on with quiet grace,
With memories I can't erase.
She taught me more than she could know,
That hearts must bloom and not outgrow.

So now I guard my inner land,
With cautious eyes and gentler hand.
For letting someone near your soul,
Can bless or break the self you hold.

Let this be written in my lore,
That love unshared still shakes the core.
And even when we choose what's right,
It doesn't always end in light.

Chapter – XX
Ashes Of An Unheard Heart

"When kindness grew claws."

What began as warmth turned bitter and raw, she loved like a rose, but her hands held claws.

Chapter – XX: Ashes Of An Unheard Heart

When Love Turns Into Fire

I never meant to dim a flame,
I spoke with care, not cruel blame.
A gentle "no," an honest light,
Yet it turned her day into night.

She once stood near with soul so kind,
A friend I thought was pure in mind.
But when I could not love her back,
The warmth she gave began to crack.

Affection once that gently flowed,
Now burned in glances sharp and cold.
The heart that bloomed with tender grace,
Now sought to scorch my sacred space.

She said, "If not with me, then none,"
A vow that blocked the rising sun.
She could not bear another hand,
To hold the joy she once had planned.

I saw the shift, from friend to foe,
From whispered care to ruthless woe.
It hurt to watch a soul so sweet,
Turn bitter with each step I meet.

But I stood still, I did not bend,
For I had truth as my defense.
She launched her fire, her silent war,
But I had walked through worse before.

They say revenge is love denied,
But it's the love that's gone awry.
And though she tried to scar my name,
Her shadows broke against my flame.

I never feared her threat or pain,
For storms can't drown a soul with flame.
An old soul knows that hearts can fall,
But truth will outlast hate and all.

I learned a lesson hard and clear,
That even friends can bring you fear.
That closeness, if not watched with grace,
Can turn into a darker place.

I do not blame, I do not curse,
Her silence now speaks even worse.
I only pray her wounds will mend,
And not become the means to end.

But me, I walk with truth held high,
Beneath an honest, open sky.
For though her arrows sought to bend,
It's truth that guards me in the end.

So now I smile, though scarred within,
With strength that truth carved deep in skin.
She tried to break what she once knew,
But couldn't touch the core so true.

Chapter - XXI
Untamed And Alive

"Two wild flames that lit the dark."

We burned like stars not meant to stay, untamed and alive, then drifted away.

Chapter – XXI: Untamed And Alive

Wild Hearts, Quiet Goodbyes

I had seen the highs and known the lows,
From love that bloomed to pain that grows.
I walked on glass, I loved with care,
Till one bold soul lit fire from air.

She came not soft, nor cloaked in grace,
But with wild winds across her face.
She said, "No chains, no vows to keep,
Just moments wide and oceans deep."

A warrior heart, untamed and true,
She taught me things I never knew.
Not love in silk, but flames that bite,
A kiss that sparked electric night.

I never kissed the girl I had loved,
But here I kissed and stars above
Exploded in our reckless skies,
Two hearts not tame enough for lies.

She passed me smoke with steady hands,
And pulled me into fearless lands.
I was afraid, she said, "Just try,"
And so we flew where rules can't fly.

One day she asked, "Let's end in bed,"
I paused, a storm within my head.
I said, "Not yet," but deep inside,
Our blood was young and wild with pride.

She took me home, she served me there,
But her mother's eyes were hard to bear.
She came to mine, she smiled, she ate,
But fate grew tired and came too late.

We dreamed of vows, we said, "Let's wed,"
But dreams can fade when words go dead.
She loved me fierce, she loved me fast,
But some wild loves are not meant to last.

She taught me touch, she taught me thrill,
She showed me scars, and loved me still.
Not for the man I had to be,
But for the soul she dared to see.

We didn't end in bridal song,
But danced in memories all along.
No bitter fight, no angry cries,
Just one long hug beneath the skies.

Some loves don't come with rings and names,
They come with stars and wildfire flames.
And though they burn, and leave no trace,
They leave a warmth you can't replace.

So here I stand, not draped in shame,
But proud I played her fearless game.
For she was wild, and I was new,
We wrote a story bold and true.

No promises, no "ever after,"
Just reckless nights and untamed laughter.
And when I think of where we've been,
We gave our souls and called it sin.

Chapter - XXII
The Teacher Who Saw My Soul

"Lessons beyond the black board."

She entered my life with lessons and grace, but healed the pain no words could replace.

Chapter – XXII: The Teacher Who Saw My Soul

The Chalk That Rewrote My Story

I spoke less to the world outside,
As final pages were blurred and dried.
When friendships cracked in jealous flame,
A teacher came and changed the game.

She was not just chalk and board,
But someone I silently adored.
Not a lover, not a flame,
But still, she knew me, just the same.

She was young, yet held such light,
A friend who saw my wrong and right.
We shared our meals, we shared our days,
In silent care, in subtle praise.

I spoke to her what none could hear,
My wounds, my dreams, my shade, my cheer.
She listened soft, with no demand,
And held my world with open hand.

We never crossed a reckless line,
But oh, how close our souls aligned.
She said one day with wistful smile,
"If you were older by a while."

Her voice, so soft, like rain in spring,
"I would've worn your wedding ring."
I laughed, but hid the quiet ache,
For hearts sometimes are meant to break.

She wasn't mine, and I knew why,
But still I wished beneath the sky.
That in some life, in some odd year,
Our love could bloom, so pure, so clear.

She gave me strength, she left her mark,
She saw my light beyond the dark.
I outperformed, I led my class,
But only she knew why I rose.

We weren't a couple in the rain,
But danced through joy and shared the pain.
No kiss was there, no vow to bind,
Just two whole hearts, so intertwined.

She was the wind I couldn't hold,
A story soft, yet never told.
She wasn't perfect, but she was true,
And left a mark none ever knew.

And when she left, she left no scar,
Just distance drawn by fate too far.
Yet even now, I close my eyes,
And feel her in my midnight skies.

We knew our hearts, we knew our roles,
We walked away with honoured souls.
Not every love is loud or grand,
Some hold your life, then leave your hand.

But still I rise, with strength she gave,
And write her name on every wave.
For teachers come and then they part,
But some remain inside your heart.

Chapter - XXIII
The Weight Of Want

"Becoming the bones that wouldn't break."

When want became a weight I refused to drop, that weight became a will that would never stop.

Chapter – XXIII: The Weight Of Want

The Burden Of Becoming

I once believed that life was slow,
Dreams just bloom and freely grow.
But time, that teacher none escapes,
Revealed the truth in shifting shapes.

As days turned old and youth turned wise,
I saw through hope's half-painted skies.
People came like wind and left like rain,
But duty stayed, both gift and chain.

I wished one day to drive with pride,
To feel the wind and roads collide.
A car, so simple, yet so wide,
A dream I held but tried to hide.

My mother's hands, once laced with gold,
Were traded in for dreams I hold.
She gave her jewels, her quiet grace,
And placed my longing in that space.

I saw her smile, yet felt the cost,
The years she wore, the shine she lost.
And so I swore, on bended knee,
"This debt, I'll pay to thee."

College days with weary tread,
Intern by dawn, by dusk I fed.
Each evening shift, a quiet art,
To stitch my love into her heart.

While peers grew bitter, envy-born,
I left at dusk, returned past morn.
Their whispers stung, but I stayed still,
For dreams are carved by greater will.

I walked with moon, not friends, not fame,
My shoes were tired, but not my flame.
No time to rest, no nights to spare,
Just silent grit and midnight prayer.

Then came a storm, the world went black,
As COVID cast its heavy track.
My father's work, it disappeared,
And hunger's shadow came too near.

But through my sweat, the fire I bore,
My family fed, we lacked no more.
And in that hour, I understood,
That pain can sometimes birth the good.

What once I chased to feel alive,
Became the means for us to survive.
And in that trade, the truth rang clear,
Desire speaks soft, but costs sincere.

A wish is not a whispered breeze,
But born in storms on trembling knees.
It bears the weight of silent cries,
It walks through fire before it flies.

And still I stand, though time has flown,
With scars that only I have known.
I've learned God sees beyond our sight,
And holds us fast in secret light.

So, if you dream, then brace your soul,
For dreams demand a deeper role.
They test your faith, they burn your pride,
But walk with God, and He'll provide.

Desire is a fire wrapped in grace,
It burns the heart, yet lights the place.
And though it feeds on pain each day,
It blooms through sweat in quiet sway.

Chapter - XXIV
The House My Mother Deserved

"It wasn't a house I built, it was a promise I kept."

Brick by brick, I rebuilt her grace, a love once hidden in a silent place. She gave me dreams while hunger stayed, now I give her a roof, where thanks are laid.

Chapter – XXIV: The House My Mother Deserved

Home On The Edge Of Hope

Everyone dreams of a place to belong,
A corner of earth, a roof, a song.
Not made of marble, not dressed in pride,
Just peace in walls, and love inside.

But mine was born in blood and fight,
In lanes where day would fear the night.
Where rage ran wild, and silence screamed,
And murder walked where children dreamed.

A slum of smoke, where crimes would breed,
Where gold meant guns and soul would bleed.
But still I dreamed of something more,
A door my mom could call her door.

We owned some land, a sacred piece,
But selling it gave no release.
For kindness hid in cunning's clothes,
And poison bloomed where money grows.

My mother wept, but still was strong,
While deals went crooked, cruel, and wrong.
Yet I held tight and made a vow,
"I'll build our home, I just don't know how."

I sold our land, my only stake,
But dreams don't always sweetly wake.
For all I had, in cities tall,
Was barely dust, was worth so small.

We stood alone on empty street,
No path ahead, no ground beneath.
But I looked at her, and she at me,
And said, "One day, you'll set us free."

So I searched the skies, I searched the stone,
I searched the world to make us home.
When man denied and maps misled,
I turned my cries to God instead.

And there it was, as still as grace,
A house that wore a calm embrace.
Beside a lake, the breeze would hum,
Like lullabies from heaven come.

The waves would kiss the quiet shore,
As if they knew what we fought for.
And there I stood, with teary pride,
With mom and dreams by water's side.

It wasn't grand, it didn't shine,
But in its peace, I saw a sign.
For this was not a house alone,
It was a place our soul had known.

The pain we'd borne, the nights we cried,
Were buried there, but not denied.
They built the ground on which we stood,
A story made from broken wood.

So when they ask what bricks I laid,
I say, "The ones my mother prayed."
For what we found was not just space,
But silence dressed in God's own grace.

A home, at last, not bought by wealth,
But by a son who gave his health.
And if I fall, or rise again,
That home will hold my joy and pain.

I brought her back what we had sold,
Not in silver, but in soul.
And now we sit with peace and tea,
By the lake, just her and me.

Chapter - XXV
Echoes Of Friendship, Lessons Of Reality

"Not all bonds are meant to last; some are meant to teach."

I lost my friendships, but found my ground. In the echoes of silence, success was found.

Chapter – XXV: Echoes Of Friendship, Lessons Of Reality

The Silence After Success

As days grew old and nights grew tight,
I chased the dawn; I lost the light.
Life pulled me in with hands so wide,
And left no space for those beside.

Once I would laugh, once I would stay,
But bread had to be earned each day.
My hands were full, my eyes were worn,
And friendships thinned like threads well-torn.

My teacher, once my soul's own twin,
Whispered, "You don't love like you did back then."
And though I tried, I gave it all,
But love grew quiet at duty's call.

I didn't leave for joy or pride,
I left to keep my dreams alive.
I spoke to fewer, called back late,
And bonds, like dew, evaporate.

The talks we had, the jokes, the grace,
All faded slow without a trace.
They thought I changed, forgot, let go,
But I was busy building hope.

I was saving homes through sleepless fight,
While losing mine in fading light.
And purpose grew like silent fire,
But doused the warmth of old desire.

I walked away from every laugh,
With heavy steps on golden path.
Success arrived in wealth and name,
But no one left to call the same.

I stood atop the dream I drew,
With empty chairs and sky so blue.
The trophies gleamed, the silence too,
And not a soul to say, “I’m proud of you.”

When I had none, the room was warm,
With broken hearts that braved the storm.
Now I have all, but feel the chill,
Of vacant hearts and windows still.

I fed the world, but starved my own,
I built a throne but sit alone.
And now I know what growth can cost,
A thousand gains for one love lost.

So if you rise, rise soft, rise true,
Don’t let the light forget the you
That laughed for hours and cried with friends,
For journeys hurt that never bend.

But still I rise, not bound in pain,
For love, once lost, still leaves a stain.
A memory sweet, a lesson deep,
To sow the joy you one day reap.

And if you climb, just turn and see,
The ones who walked your past with glee.
For life is short, and dreams are tall,
But love, once gone, that's the deepest fall.

Chapter - XXVI
Four Paws That Loved Me Back

"The Heart That Found Me When No One Else Did."

Silence echoed through my tale, till love arrived with a wagging tail. In fur and warmth, I found my part, a quiet paw stitched back my heart.

Chapter – XXVI: Four Paws That Loved Me Back

When Love Had Four Legs

I grew in silence, not in song,
Among the crowd, I felt so wrong.
No human arms gave me their grace,
But four small paws, a furry face.

She wasn't bought from any place,
She came from roads, from pain and chase.
A black stray pup with eyes so wide,
Brave as a lion, with love as her guide.

She looked at me, not just as "boy,"
But as her world, her peace, her joy.
From hall to bed, from dusk to dawn,
She stayed with me, her leash was gone.

We ate as one, we slept as kin,
She knew each ache that burned within.
No words exchanged, no need to try,
She read my soul through every sigh.

Each night she waited by the gate,
Through wind and dusk, through rain and fate.
And when I stepped into my door,
She touched my feet, my heart, much more.

Not even Ma would greet me first,
She'd reach me fast, with love that burst.
She kissed my pain, she chewed my scars,
She made me feel I came from stars.

But joy and love don't last for long,
Life finds its way to prove you wrong.
My mother's health began to wane,
She wheezed and coughed; she spoke of pain.

The doctor said, "It's her or you,"
My world went dark, my spirit too.
And she once asked through teary blur,
"Do you want me or still want her?"

A dagger pierced my trembling chest,
For both were homes where I found rest.
But blood must choose the older vow,
I chose my mom, I'm broken now.

I took her back where I first found
Her lonely steps on thorny ground.
And when I tried to walk away,
She broke her chain and ran astray.

She jumped on me and didn't bark,
Her eyes were oceans, deep and dark.
We didn't speak, we couldn't lie,
Just soul to soul, and cry to cry.

I hugged her tight, she wagged no more,
As if she knew what stood before.
She licked my face and sat in peace,
Like saying, "Go, I'll find release."

The hardest part is still today,
I see her ghost in every way.
The sound of paws, the empty bed,
The dreams we shared, now left unsaid.

But here's the truth I came to know:
Not all who love will always show.
Some angels walk not with a wing,
But tails that wag, and hearts that sing.

Chapter – XXVII When Love Wasn't Enough

"They saw my soul, but searched for silver, at the altar of love, I was priced, not embraced."

I came with love, not silver or gold, but they wanted wealth, not stories untold. My heart was full, my hands were bare, and still they judged what wasn't there.

Chapter – XXVII: When Love Wasn't Enough

Altar Of Hope, Walls Of Greed

I walked this world with wounds still bare,
With dreams that bled in silent prayer.
From broken ground, I learned to rise,
And chase the dawn through shadowed skies.

I stood with arms outstretched and bare,
A heart uncloaked, a soul laid there.
For love, for truth, for sacred ties,
I faced the unknown path with open eyes.

They came with names, with silver talk,
With shallow eyes that watched me walk.
But when they heard my tale, my truth,
They turned away, denied my youth.

No one asked how kind I had been,
Or what I've faced or felt within.
No one searched for soul or scars,
They searched my worth in cars and jars.

They measured love in family name,
In caste, in cash, in social fame.
Not once did they ask, “Can he love right?”
Just, “Does he own enough for flight?”

One father said, “He burns with flame,”
But she still looked and spoke with shame,
“I’d marry you if gold you brought,
But I can’t live on just your thought.”

Her voice was calm, her heart was cold,
She left me there, bruised but bold.
“I like your light,” she softly said,
“But not enough to share your bread.”

And so I smiled, though deep it hurt,
And brushed my soul out of the dirt.
I told myself, with quiet might,
“No more I beg for borrowed light.”

If I must climb a steeper wall,
Then I will rise or I will fall.
But till I build the life I dream,
I won’t beg love that lacks esteem.

Not till I reach where I deserve,
Will I let my spirit swerve.
I won't kneel low for hollow hands,
Or break for hearts with shifting stands.

Let them choose by name and race,
Let them chase a wealthier face.
But I'll keep walking, true and clear,
With love that waits, not ruled by fear.

So if they ask why I delay,
Tell them this, without dismay:
"He's not for sale, he's not for show,
He'll marry when his truth can grow."

And one day, she will walk in light,
Not for my crown, but for my fight.
She'll love the man, not just his place,
And choose my soul, not just my face.

Chapter - XXVIII
A Wedding Without Tomorrow

"Dressed in dreams, undone by fury and fumes."

No vows were said, no garlands thrown, yet in that silence, I stood alone.

Chapter – XXVIII: A Wedding Without A Tomorrow

Where Vows Were Ready, But Fate Was Not

We crossed the paths where fate once stood,
Where talks of "forever" felt so good.
She said, "I'll walk this life with you,"
And stars above felt soft and true.

Our names were carved in plans so bright,
With blessings cast in morning light.
Two hearts that rose from different stone,
Still dared to dream a love full-grown.

She worshipped gods in sculpted clay,
While I lit candles where I pray.
But still, we met with soul not skin,
And hoped a life could now begin.

The families met, the talk was made,
The wedding cards were freshly laid.
We laughed, we dreamt, we danced, we planned,
Together with the world in hand.

And then I said, “Let’s make it right,
The first card must be God's delight.”
So with my mother by my side,
We walked into the temple wide.

“Give me the card,” I softly said,
She searched her bag, then shook her head.
No card was there. No note. No proof.
Just silence hung beneath the roof.

I stood in shock, my soul went cold,
A crack had formed I couldn’t hold.
We laughed it off, but deep inside,
The winds of truth refused to hide.

An old astrologer had warned,
“This match may leave your spirit torn.”
But blinded by the dreams we drew,
We brushed aside what could be true.

Three days remained before we wed,
But hearts grew sharp with words we said.
A silly fight, a broken thread,
And vows dissolved in pain and dread.

She went her way, I walked mine too,
Two rings exchanged, now lost in blue.
No altar met our trembling feet,
Just echoes of a love incomplete.

It wasn't lies that tore us down,
But truths we hadn't fully known.
A love that bloomed, but couldn't stay,
A wedding dream that slipped away.

Yet from this ache, I found my core,
I closed that door to search for more.
Not in a bride, not in a name,
But in the man I must reclaim.

For some events don't end in cheer,
But plant the truths we need to hear.
And though the sky refused to shine,
The stars still shaped this fate of mine.

So now I stand, not lost, not torn,
But wiser from the love that mourned.
A wedding that had no tomorrow,
till carved a path through grief and sorrow.

Chapter - XXIX
Turning Pain Into Power

"Each scar became a sword."

They tried to end me with silence and flame, but I rose from the ashes, no longer the same.

Chapter – XXIX: Turning Pain Into Power

The Rise After Ruin

The wedding broke before the vow,
And I was left to wonder how,
How dreams can die before they start,
And leave a crater in the heart.

No shoulders there to hold my fall,
No voice to hear my silent call.
I wiped my tears and wore a smile,
And walked to work though crushed the while.

I asked for leave, a breath, a break,
But they just said, "Don't sit and ache."
I stepped inside with pain unspoken,
But every breath was bruised and broken.

My boss then snapped, "Leave pain at gate,"
As if my grief had no just weight.
They promised pay, they gave me lies,
And watched me drown with hollow eyes.

I gave my sweat, I gave my name,
But when I left, they played a game.
No notice served, no handshake grace,
Just silence thrown back in my face.

And so, I sat, jobless, alone,
With rent to pay, and bills I own.
Thirty days that felt like years,
Each moment soaked in silent tears.

But God still watched, and fate still stirred,
And through the dark, I heard a word.
A stranger came, a guide so kind,
And dropped a flame into my mind.

"You're built for more than what you do,
There's greater power locked in you.
Don't chase the path that left you bruised,
Make pain your sword, not just your wound."

So I looked in, not out, for worth,
And saw the fire I held since birth.
Not in my grade, not in degree,
But in the soul the world would see.

With every quote I once had penned,
With posts that helped a stranger mend,
A manager saw my silent flame,
And called me in, and spoke my name.

Not marks, not ranks, not test or score,
But presence that could shake the floor.
They hired the heart, not just the face,
And gave my wounds a brand new place.

So now I stand, not where I planned,
But in a land I did not demand.
And every tear they made me shed,
Became the ink by which I bled.

I learned that pain is not the end,
It's just the curve before you bend.
And though they broke what I had grown,
I found a crown I forged alone.

If they should break your tender wings,
Remember what the fire brings.
From every ash, a soul can rise,
Not just to live, but claim the skies.

Chapter - XXX
A New Beginning

"The end that set me free."

Where old pain bowed, and new purpose bloomed. No longer fighting to survive, I simply stepped into being alive.

Chapter – XXX: A New Beginning

Born Again In Silence And Sunlight

In lands unknown, I found my grace,
A quiet smile, a softer pace.
The past still wept behind my eyes,
But here, I saw new morning skies.

New faces came, with hands held wide,
No judgment cast, no need to hide.
They saw not scars but strength within,
And let my second life begin.

I trained the minds, I touched the soul,
Each word I spoke had earned its toll.
They saw in me a silent spark,
That once was lost inside the dark.

The field was new, the craft untried,
But still I stood, and never lied.
With every task, with every test,
I gave my heart, I gave my best.

They watched in awe as I would grow,
From roots of ash to morning glow.
And not just in the world so near,
But online too, my name drew cheer.

On virtual sands, I carved my name,
Not chasing fame, but building flame.
With every post, with every share,
I proved that pain births those who dare.

I worked beyond the ticking time,
Each hour unpaid, each climb sublime.
I stayed back late, I knelt to learn,
From every elder, every turn.

Even one lesson, small or deep,
I'd hold like treasure I must keep.
They taught, I bowed, I learned with pride,
For now, I had no need to hide.

A mentor came, whose light I knew,
I stood with him, so firm, so true.
I bore his tasks, his mission made,
With silent strength and no charade.

Though secret roles were never mine,
Still I rose, and still I shine.
Not from shortcuts, not from schemes,
But from sweat and sleepless dreams.

A star was born not in the night,
But in the wounds that chose the light.
The child once broken, mocked, and bruised,
Now wore the crown the world refused.

And so I say to those who ache,
Let not your faith or hands forsake.
For when you rise from shattered clay,
Your hard work carves the brightest day.

Chapter - XXXI
Search Of Love

"I searched the silence for her name, but only echoes ever came."

I searched for her in silence deep, and found my love where verses sleep. So, I held a pen with quiet grace, and loved her through the page's space.

Chapter – XXXI: Search Of Love

When I Couldn't Find Her Hand, I Held A Pen

When I was young, just flesh and flame,
I searched for love and whispered name.
In every glance, in every face,
I looked for home, for warm embrace.

A boy still tender, raw and wide,
With storms of longing trapped inside.
I saw a wife in every smile,
A future shaped in every mile.

My heart was soft, my hopes ran high,
But truth would often pass me by.
They came and went, like fleeting rain,
Yet none could wash away my pain.

I spoke with care, I walked them through,
I dreamt of love both deep and true.
But race and class would draw the line,
And love was sold, not made divine.

Some offered hearts, some spoke in verse,
But something missed, a silent curse.
They loved the name, they loved the flame,
But not the soul behind my name.

And so I wandered, year by year,
With empty hands and eyes sincere.
My arms once stretched to find a bride,
Now held a pen and wrote with pride.

What I could not give to one,
Was shared in poems softly spun.
My love, rejected by the world,
In every stanza now unfurled.

Each verse I wrote, a piece of me,
A wound disguised as poetry.
And people paused, and people read,
And through my ink, my love had bled.

Not just for one, but all who ache,
For hearts too soft the world will break.
They saw my pain, they felt my fire,
My words became what they desire.

For I was more than boy denied,
I was a river not yet dried.
And though no arms had held me tight,
My verses danced through every night.

And now I love with wiser eyes,
Not chasing hands or shallow ties.
For love is more than just a vow,
It's how you heal, not just the how.

So if she comes, she'll find me whole,
Not begging heart, but blooming soul.
For I have found a deeper way,
To love the world through words I lay.

No hand to hold, no voice to trace,
Just silence dressed in her embrace.
In quiet ink, I bled my ache,
Each word a scar I chose to make.

I searched for her in silent lines,
And found my heart between the rhymes.
So I held a pen instead of her hand,
And loved her where the words would land.

Chapter - XXXII
Left The Fire Behind

"The battle wasn't her to fight, but
she ignited all my night."

Not every flame is meant to warm, some only sear the soul with harm. I walked from love's relentless fire, to find the calm my scars desire.

Chapter – XXXII: Left The Fire Behind

I Heard My Heart, Walked Away

I walked alone with a heart grown wide,
Searching for love, not lust in disguise.
But fate had plans both sharp and strange,
A woman came, and winds did change.

She wasn't mine, nor I was hers,
Yet hearts can blur when silence stirs.
She smiled with warmth, her eyes like flame,
And softly, sweetly, spoke my name.

She said, "Even married hearts can sway,
When men like you just pass their way."
Her words were silk, her voice was balm,
Yet every glance would steal my calm.

We spoke for hours, the world stood still,
But in my chest, grew war and will.
She lit a fire I'd never known,
But it burned a soul I thought was grown.

I told her once, "come walk with me,
I'll give you love and set you free."
But still she stayed with vows once sworn,
And I was left both torn and worn.

How could this be if love was true?
Why did her hands hold more than two?
She kept her world, and texted mine,
And I stood trapped between the lines.

The ache was deep, the guilt ran wide,
I saw my faith begin to slide.
No touch had crossed, yet hearts had strayed,
And silent shame inside me stayed.

One night I called, with breaking tone,
"My soul is bruised, I feel alone.
This isn't right, we both must part,
Before we burn the sacred heart."

She heard the storm behind my breath,
And understood the weight beneath.
She wept a while, but then agreed,
That love like this was laced in need.

We left that bond, we left that fire,
We buried dreams we once admired.
No blame, no hate, just truth untold,
A story paused before it stole.

And though she left, the flame stayed near,
A test of strength, a test of fear.
But from that fire, I walked away,
A man more whole, more strong that day.

No woman since could breach my soul,
No eyes could take what she once stole.
For in her trial, I found my grace,
A holy fire I chose to face.

I didn't win by touch or kiss,
I won by choosing what I would miss.
To rise above what pulls us down,
To earn not lust, but Heaven's crown.

So if you ask what forged my name,
It wasn't fame, it wasn't flame.
It was the night I turned from desire,
And left behind that raging fire.

Now blood divine flows through my vein,
Where once there lived both thrill and pain.
And though she taught me how to feel,
It's God who taught me how to heal.

Chapter - XXXIII
My Chosen Soul

"She was a destiny wrapped in my soul."

She wasn't just a chapter in my life; she was the ink that wrote me whole. A love that carved my soul.

Chapter – XXXIII: My Chosen Soul

The Soul I Called My Own

She wasn't found in halls of gold,
Nor in the tales the scholars told.
She didn't rise from cheer or fame,
She bloomed in verse and spoke my name.

She rose from ink I never planned,
A stranger drawn by poet's hand.
She touched the verse, then touched my fate,
And in her eyes, I saw my gate.

A soul unknown, yet felt so near,
She walked from poems into my year.
A reader first, with rhythm's grace,
But love soon bloomed from written space.

She came as light in letters deep,
Where silence once had learned to sleep.
Each word I wrote, she heard it whole,
And in that verse, she found my soul.

We spoke through dusk, we spoke through dawn,
While every ache and void were gone.
From night's first star to morning's hue,
We built a world in words we knew.

Her voice was soft, like twilight rain,
It touched my soul and eased the pain.
And when she asked, "Will you walk with me?"
I vowed, "Through fire, through sky, through sea."

We loved before our eyes had met,
A bond so fierce, our soul's won't forget.
We vowed to stand through light and dark,
Two burning names, one blazing spark.

And when we met in shadow's hour,
It bloomed like night's forbidden flower.
She came so close, no fear, no shame,
And whispered love inside my name.

She kissed me once, and time stood still,
A rush, a hush, a sacred thrill.
Her heart pressed deep against my chest,
As if to say, "Here is your rest."

It wasn't lust, it went too far,
It felt like touching who we are.
Like lifetimes passed in single breath,
A love too bold to bow to death.

The stars stood witness to our flame,
The skies repeated just one name.
For we were forged in soul, not skin,
And felt the fire from deep within.

She tested me, yet I stood true,
Not just as man, but soulmate too.
And in that night where flesh met grace,
I saw God smiling through her face.

We aren't just lovers bound by time,
We echo through eternity's rhyme.
From birth to dust, from breath to star,
Our hearts remain, just where they are.

We weren't just lovers here and now,
We'd met before, I don't know how.
From life to life, from birth to breath,
We walk together, past all death.

So if I die, this tale won't break,
It echoes through each soul I wake.
We weren't just lovers cast in skin,
We were the home love carved within.

So if they ask what love is called,
It's not a game, it's not enthralled.
It's finding home in someone's breath,
And choosing them through life and death.

She is my chosen, carved by flame,
Not just in body, soul, or name.
But in the space where echoes stay,
Where love won't burn, but finds its way.

She wasn't chosen from the crowd,
Her name was carved in Heaven loud.
And in each poem that I unfold,
You'll see her name, in breathless gold.

Chapter - XXXIV
Candle In The Storm

"She lit my world, right before it fell apart."

She came like a sparkle, gentle and bright, a silent miracle in my endless night. When I was left in the dark, she was the one who lit the spark.

Chapter – XXXIV: Candle In The Storm

Her Love Held My Scattered Soul

I've walked through life with weary feet,
Met many souls, both kind and sweet.
But not a soul, in all my days,
Made love feel safe in softer ways.

Till she arrived, with silent grace,
A northern star in southern place.
No maps, no roads could guide our way,
But hearts don't ask, they just obey.

She didn't shine with worldly light,
She was a candle in my night.
When storms would scream and spirits fall,
Her presence rose above it all.

Her lap became my peaceful land,
Her bosom calmed my trembling hand.
Her arms, a place where wars could cease,
Where broken hearts could breathe in peace.

She held me not in fleeting thrill,
But in a vow both fierce and still.
And in her chest, I heard a tone,
A heartbeat whispering, "You're own."

We shared our wounds, our shame, our scars,
We kissed beneath forgotten stars.
In darkest nights, with curtains drawn,
We spoke of silence until the dawn.

She touched my mother's feet with grace,
And brought a smile upon her face.
No games, no pride, no mask, no show,
Just truth in tears we let each other know.

She wasn't just a girl I chose,
She was the garden where my love grows.
I crowned her heart, she wore it proud,
With her heart pounding loud.

Together we had built a song,
In days too short and nights too long.
Through tide and time, through ache and air,
We loved like none else ever dare.

But some tales end before they're told,
Even strong hearts can break and fold.
And though our story stayed unsaid,
She burned within me, soft and red.

Not every fire burns to ash,
Some live forever in each flash.
Of memory held, of dreams once sown,
Of hands once touched and roots once grown.

We weren't just bodies in a room,
We were two souls that dared to bloom.
And if the world would tear us wide,
Our promise still would walk beside.

I'll love her still through shifting fate,
Beyond the locks, beyond the gate.
For in my soul, she lit a flame,
That burns beyond both form and name.

She wasn’t just a fleeting flame,
She was the prayer I couldn’t name.
And though some paths may lead alone,
I’ll carry her in my heart as my own.

Chapter - XXXV
Scars Beneath The Silence

"Some scars don't scream; they whisper beneath the silence."

Not all pain speaks in cries or screams, some dwells in silent dreams. The story I never said, and the one that still haunts me when I lay in bed.

Chapter – XXXV: Scars Beneath The Silence

The Loudest Ache Of My Soul

We started love when nights were long,
With trembling steps, not voices strong.
In darkest hours, we lit our flame,
And gave our hearts without a name.

Time passed by like silent stream,
And life bestowed a fleeting dream.
A symbol came, so small, so light,
A spark of us, a soul so bright.

But she, the one my heart adored,
Was not prepared to walk that chord.
She chose to let the silence win,
To bury what had bloomed within.

I begged in prayers, I wept alone,
For flesh of mine, for blood and bone.
I tied her soul with sacred thread,
In hope she'd stay, not run, not dread.

But still she chose the darker door,
And left me aching at the core.
She walked away, her heart held tight,
While I was pierced in quiet night.

The one we lost, it haunts me still,
It whispers soft against my will.
It asks me why I didn't fight,
Why love gave up without a light.

No stone was carved, no name was said,
Just ashes where a soul had bled.
No farewell song, no final cry,
Just echoes in the midnight sky.

That loss became a shadow, a stain,
A silent scar beneath my pain.
A wound unseen, a vow undone,
A chapter burned before begun.

In silent hours, we sometimes trace
The shadow of love in empty space.
Not born, not gone, not touched or said,
But breathing where the soul has bled.

And yet, she held me once again,
With eyes that wept and arms like rain.
She kissed the ache, she calmed the roar,
Though nothing was the same as before.

We cried not just for what we lost,
But for the hearts we paid in cost.
And standing tall through broken grace,
We found the strength to still embrace.

Some love survives the cruellest fate,
Some bonds grow stronger through the weight.
And though that soul is far from near,
Its light still lingers in our tear.

So here we are, not whole, but true,
Still walking life with pain in view.
And though that silence scars us deep,
It taught us how the brave ones weep.

We're not made less by what we bear,
But shaped by how we choose to care.
And in the dark where sorrow grew,
We touched the light and rose anew.

We are not whole, we are not right,
But still we stand in candlelight.
Two souls with cracks that moonlight fills,
Still holding hands on haunted hills.

Chapter - XXXVI
Climbing Dreams, Scar By Scar

"Where pain was the ladder, and scars lit the climb."

I climbed not because I was whole, but because my scars had shaped my soul. I climbed on pieces of my pain, and found the light beyond the rain.

Chapter – XXXVI: Climbing Dreams, Scar By Scar

Built From Pain, Fueled By Hope

I gave my heart, I gave my flame,
To serve with truth, not chase for fame.
With every breath, I built with care,
But found betrayal in the air.

They smiled and spoke of future bright,
Of honours grand, of golden light.
They dressed me up in awards and fame,
But left my soul without a name.

They promised more, but gave me less,
And wrapped me tight in silent stress.
No hands to lift, no truth to share,
Just hollow praise and vacant stare.

They took my time, they drained my youth,
And shattered all I called my truth.
And when I asked for simple grace,
They turned away, no saving face.

My health grew frail, my fire dimmed,
The light I bore began to swim.
I stood alone in darkest hour,
A wilting rose with fading power.

But still I rose, not loud, not fast,
With wisdom carved from every past.
With grace no words could steal or fake,
I walked away for my soul's sake.

They tried to hold me with regret,
With empty words and quiet debt.
But I, who once had bowed and bled,
Stood tall and softly shook my head.

I said, "No more, I've paid the price,
With sleepless nights and sacrifice.
I choose my peace, I choose my breath,
I choose my life, not silent death."

And fate, like wind, began to blow,
To newer lands where stars could grow.
Where worth was not just lips and lies,
But seen with truth in open eyes.

I climbed again with silent pace,
With scarred feet wrapped in quiet grace.
Each step a wound, each wound a stair,
Each fall a lesson shaped in prayer.

And now I stand where light feels right,
Not dimmed by doubt, but full in sight.
They may have crowned me late, it's true,
But I was always passing through.

So, if you ask what made me rise,
It wasn't praise or perfect skies.
It was the day I stood in pain,
And chose to rise again, again.

Chapter - XXXVII Touched Thousands With One Truth

"I did not just teach minds, I lit souls."

When fame found my name, I stood without a pause. I stood for the crowd and truth was my cause.

Chapter – XXXVII: Touched Thousands With One Truth

Not For Applause, But For Purpose

I walked alone where none had shown,
With only will and aching bone.
I stumbled first, then learned to rise,
Till stars began to seek my skies.

From pain I rose, through wounds and wars,
And now I stand beneath their stars.
A thousand hearts lift up their gaze,
And stood there to light the blaze.

I wasn't loud, I wasn't grand,
But wisdom rested in my hand.
Not just with words or classroom walls,
But with the way my silence calls.

They called me "sir," they called me "guide,"
But I just stood there, arms open wide.
Not giving facts or marks to chase,
But truth, and hope, and gentle grace.

Some came to me with dreams half-dead,
I fed them fire and light instead.
Some came with pride, some came in pain,
But all walked out with something gained.

I gave not only flame, but glow,
A light to guide when winds would blow.
And though they flew where I've not gone,
They carry stars my hands had drawn.

So many came and crossed my gate,
Some rushed by time, some slowed by fate.
Their names dissolved like grains of sand,
But I still feel each soul, each hand.

What's built within a silent soul
Will outlast crowns or scripted scroll.
And those who touched my humble shore
Now walk with truth forevermore.

One truth I gave, one steady flame,
And still, they speak aloud my name.
Not for the lessons, chalk or test,
But for the love I gave the rest.

Though time now flies like winds unbound,
The roots we grew still hold the ground.
They called me star, I bore it true,
Not for acclaim, but for what I knew.

But for the quiet lives I reached,
For every heart my silence preached.
The one who once had lost his way,
Now lights the world in brighter day.

And if I leave, or fade from sight,
I'll go in peace; I was their light.
I touched a thousand, gave my youth,
And lit their paths with just one truth.

Chapter - XXXVIII
A Mentor Was Born, Not Made

"I did not just teach minds, I lit souls."

Not born with chalk in a steady hand, but with a heart that could understand. Great teachers are carved, not merely planned.

Chapter – XXXVIII: A Mentor Was Born, Not Made

In Their Tie, I Became A Guide

I walked into halls with fire in my eyes,
A voice like thunder, yet calm as the skies.
Young and bold, with dreams untamed,
But never seeking wealth or fame.

I spoke with light, I stood with truth,
And walked the road that shapes our youth.
While many chased desire or gold,
I gave away my heart untold.

They came to me, those hearts unsure,
With crushes soft and glances pure.
But I had crossed that ocean wide,
Where lust once danced, now love would guide.

Their eyes would shine when I would speak,
And some would blush with joy or weak.
But I was not a fleeting flame,
I bore a torch too deep to tame.

I taught with breath, I taught with soul,
I gave my all, I gave them whole.
My voice would break, but I stood still,
A vessel moved by sacred will.

The stars were many in the night,
But I alone held constant light.
Even after dawn had stirred,
My echoes stayed, my truths were heard.

I never weighed what I would lose,
For giving all was what I'd choose.
I bled my voice to fill their minds,
I broke my sleep to light their climbs.

And slowly, like a whispered name,
They passed me on with love, not fame.
My name became a sacred thread,
A tale their hearts forever read.

They didn't praise me for a test,
But for the way I gave my best.
For how I stood till breath ran dry,
And placed their dreams above my sky.

No chalk can carve what soul can reach,
No pen can match the life I teach.
They said I wasn't just a cloud,
But silence standing strong and proud.

Not just a man who passed their way,
But music words could never say.
I was their guide, their unseen light,
The steady lamp through endless night.

And if one asks what they became,
They won't speak of titles, ranks, or name.
They'll say he gave, and gave with grace,
And lit a fire none could replace.

Chapter - XXXIX
Adoption's Grace In Silent Eyes

"A bond beyond words, a love beyond blood."

They walked this world unheard and unknown, yet left behind a heart full-grown. They never spoke but still I knew their silent love rang loud and true.

Chapter – XXXIX: Adoption's Grace

In Silent Eyes

A Yard Of Silent Souls

As days rolled on in silence deep,
I found a home where trees would sleep.
A forest's edge, the sky's own bend,
A place where broken hearts could mend.

I built no palace, no shining throne,
Just walls of peace, to rest alone.
But as I stood in nature's grace,
I saw the cries in canine face.

They came in shades of dusk and dawn,
One black, one white, one earthy brown.
Their eyes were soft, their bodies thin,
Each tail wagged pain held deep within.

They didn't bark, they didn't bite,
They just walked slow into my light.
No names they bore, no past they showed,
Just souls with stories never told.

I fed them rice with my own hand,
I cooked, I stirred, I took a stand.
They didn't want my roof or bed,
Just one warm meal and words unsaid.

Some jumped the gate, some cried to flee,
They weren't meant for captivity.
So I let go, and yet they stayed,
And in their eyes, my heart had prayed.

But peace is brief where love is raw,
For life still holds its brutal claw.
A neighbour came with leash and pet,
And cast a shadow I won't forget.

They wagged their tails, so full of cheer,
Unaware that fate was near.
A neighbour came with leash in hand,
Not knowing this was their last stand.

The road was still, the sky was gray,
No bark, no cry to light the way.
One by one, they met the end,
In silent rows, no chance to defend.

One evening dark, one poisoned ground,
The white one ate, then fell without sound.
A howl escaped into the skies,
And tore my soul with wordless cries.

Descendants gone to claws and fight,
The brown was stolen by wild night.
And black, oh black, so strong and brave,
Was beaten down yet still forgave.

The night the white one lost its breath,
I sobbed and screamed and cursed at death.
I held it close, its fur still warm,
And begged the stars to stop the storm.

I couldn't stay, the grief too wide,
The pain too loud to hold inside.
So with a bleeding heart, I left,
Of every dog, of peace, bereft.

But one remained, a quiet red,
Still wagging near the empty shed.
I kissed her head, I said goodbye,
And found a home where she could fly.

This isn't just a tale once told,
Of strays or leashes, young or old.
This is a song of bonds unspoken,
Of silent vows that can't be broken.

They didn't live to wear a name,
But left me changed, and not the same.
They showed me what it means to care,
To love without a need to share.

And now when winds brush past my door,
I hear soft paws across the floor.
And in the stars that shine above,
I see the ones who wagged their love.

Chapter - XL
Staring Into The Silence Of Death

"Where echoes end and memories begin."

Death's shadow rose without a sound, beyond all breath it pulled me down, where silence spoke and time stood blind, I heard what dying leaves behind.

Chapter – XL: Staring Into The Silence Of Death

The Loudest Pain Comes Out Without A Sound

I've walked through fire, through flame,
With broken bones and bruised-up name.
I've tasted love, I've swallowed pain,
But death, oh death, rewrote my name.

I wasn't ready for its breath,
The cold, unspoken hush of death.
Not when it came for him, the one,
Who held my soul like rising sun.

He wasn't just some fading light,
He was my shield, my silent might.
He took me up when legs gave way,
And carried all my yesterdays.

He taught me math with wrinkled hands,
And built our house with broken plans.
He walked beside me, proud, unshown,
A warrior carved in dust and bone.

But time is cruel to those who give,
It steals the breath of those who live.
He grew so still, so lost, so thin,
A war he fought just deep within.

Dementia dimmed the spark once bright,
His world grew smaller every night.
And in his eyes I saw retreat,
The man who once was thunder's beat.

One evening came, too still, too slow,
He gasped, then sighed and had to go.
I touched his face so cold, so bare,
And all I knew was silent air.

No tears came down, just blood instead,
As if my soul itself had bled.
I kissed the skin, now void of light,
Still whispering "Thank you" through the night.

They lit the pyre, he turned to flame,
And handed back what had no name.
No man, no soul, just ash and bone,
And I was left to grieve alone.

A million shards inside me fell,
As if they cracked some holy shell.
And still I hear his silent breath,
That sacred hush, the sound of death.

But even in this cruel goodbye,
He taught me how the strong must cry.
Not loud, not weak, but deep and brave,
Like standing tall beside a grave.

He didn't die, he took his place,
Among the stars, beyond this space.
And every time I break or bend,
I hear him whisper, "Rise again."

He was my roof when skies would fall,
My voice when I could barely crawl.
And now I live to honor all,
The man who stood when I was small.

So let the silence teach me still,
To walk through pain with steady will.
For though he's gone, his light remains,
A pulse that echoes in my veins.

Chapter - XLI
The Silence Between Two Souls

"Verses we couldn't voice; we loved in silence and left with no choice."

When love spoke soft but fate screamed loud, our hearts composed what time disallowed, an unspoken symphony tender and true, echoed in silence the world never knew.

Chapter – XLI: The Silence Between Two Souls

A Symphony Left Unheard

So many winds, so many days,
Life pulled us both in twisted ways.
A love once bloomed in silent air,
Now wilts beneath what wasn't fair.

I held your hand in dreams so tight,
While fate stole stars from our night.
You looked at me, your soul unsure,
And I still begged for love so pure.

I pleaded soft, I pleaded loud,
To break the cage, to make you proud.
You spoke to them with hope so thin,
But greed outweighed the love within.

They judged not heart, but wealth and name,
And lit our hopes in silent flame.
No miracle, no magic came,
Just shattered vows we couldn't claim.

You stood for them, not wrong, not right,
And I stood still and lost the fight.
I asked for faith, you gave a tear,
Then slowly disappeared from near.

Your silence screamed the loudest part,
A quiet fracture of the heart.
We spoke no lies, we meant no sin,
Yet love was drowned by blood and kin.

Our symphony, no final chord,
No closure kissed with sweet reward.
Just echoes soft of what we'd say,
If fate had let us stay that day.

But love, real love, still leaves a mark,
Even when life turns cold and dark.
It doesn't die, it just transforms,
And waits beyond the worldly norms.

We built a dream with trembling hands,
But life had drawn its stricter plans.
We weren't just lovers torn by fate,
We were two souls who came too late.

Your eyes once held the stars I sought,
But love, they said, could not be bought.
Still I stood firm, still I believed
In vows the world had never weaved.

I knocked on doors that would not bend,
I begged the sky to just defend.
I prayed your name like sacred rain,
But every drop just fell in vain.

Your lips spoke love, your heart stayed torn,
Between the roots where you were born.
You tried, I know, but not enough,
And love, by then, had lost its bluff.

Your family chose a different god,
One carved of gold, not love, not sod.
They saw my hands, not what they held,
They feared my name, the truth I spelled.

And still you stayed between the tides,
While I drowned slow as silence hides.
You didn't run, but didn't stay,
You let our heaven slip away.

You said, "I can't," and let it fade,
Like wilted vows in evening shade.
I stood and prayed for one clear voice,
But silence drowned our only choice.

So here we are, no war, no blame,
Just love that burned without a flame.
Two hearts that spoke in symphony,
Yet bound to one divided destiny.

I'll never hate, nor lay a blame,
But life has never felt the same.
A melody lost before its bloom,
A rose that vanished in its perfume.

And still I walk, with quiet grace,
Your shadow wrapped in love's embrace.
With your memory, I walk in harmony,
Still plays our Unspoken Symphony.

They ask me why my soul still aches,
It's love denied that never breaks.
To watch you choose the safer shore,
And close the door on something more.

I gave you all, I bled, I stayed,
I wrote our names where dreams were made.
But even stars can fall mid-flight,
When fear becomes the louder light.

Yet let them know, if tales are told,
I loved you loud, I loved you bold.
And though you left me in the grey,
I'd choose you still, in every way.

But some loves aren't for time to hold,
They bloom in fire, then fade in cold.
And now I walk, a quieter flame,
With half a soul that speaks your name.

And if you ache in midnight's gloom,
Still reaching for a vanished bloom,
Then know, though lost to time and sea,
You'll always be a song in me.

Chapter - XLII
Invisible Bleeding

"Each smile we wore was stitched with threads of wounds untold."

We wore a smile before the crowd, while bleeding where none were allowed. In rooms of noise, we played our part, while silence tore our soul apart.

Chapter – XLII: Invisible Bleeding

A Silent War Never Told

We parted ways, not out of will,
But from the noise that made us still.
The world around us broke apart,
What only lived inside the heart.

I tried to walk a different path,
To quiet storms, to tame the wrath.
I held new hands, but felt alone,
Each touch reminded me of home.

She too had tried to seek anew,
But every soul just felt untrue.
No laugh could match the joy we knew,
No arms could hold the way we grew.

And months went by like empty skies,
With smiles that masked the hollow cries.
Without her warmth, the world grew cold,
A wound I nursed, but never told.

Then fate, both cruel and kind inside,
Led her back to stand beside.
She heard my voice, her silence broke,
And every buried word awoke.

We wept in silence, raw and real,
For all the wounds we couldn't heal.
Each tear a whisper, each look a prayer,
For love once lost, still lingering there.

So much had passed, through fire and dust,
Through broken vows and shaken trust.
Yet love remained, it didn't fade,
Just bled beneath the pride we made.

No hand could mend what time had torn,
Yet time gave space for hearts reborn.
It pulled us through the silent trial,
To find again that sacred mile.

We faced the scars no eyes could trace,
The quiet wars we learned to face.
And though we broke in secrecy,
We rose again with soul's resiliency.

Love isn't perfect, pure, or clean,
It bleeds in places never seen.
It's choosing them through doubt and pain,
When all that's bright has slipped to rain.

And now we walk with wounds that gleam,
No longer fear within our dream.
For all we lost still helped us find,
That love like ours was deeply kind.

So, if you ask what held us fast,
It wasn't just the sacred past.
But truth that kept our spirits whole,
invisible bleeding, quiet soul to soul.

Chapter - XLIII
Second Chance In The Same Arms

"We found our way through loss and flame."

We broke, we bled, we grew apart and somehow, found our way back to the same heart.

Chapter – XLIII: Second Chance In The Same Arms

Same Touch, But New Tenderness

We drifted once, not by choice,
But by shadows drowned in louder voice.
They tore our threads with prideful might,
Yet fate stood still, and held us tight.

Through silent wars and whispered blame,
We rose again, not quite the same.
With fractured hearts that learned to burn,
We stood as one, with lessons learned.

Though life held storms, she gave me grace,
A shelter time could not erase.
Though fate had pulled our roots apart,
We bloomed again, with braver hearts.

My mother came with hopeful eyes,
A prayer, a dream, beneath the skies.
She asked, "Will you be his bride?"
The maiden smiled, but softly sighed.

"Wait a few more years," she said,
"Till paths align and fears shed."
So I became the ship to wait,
Anchored with love in my fate.

Her family stood with walls still high,
Mine reached out with trembling try.
While silence veiled their distant eyes,
We answered pain with whispered sighs.

There's pain in patience, deep and wide,
Like oceans longing for their tide.
But we were storms that knew to stay,
We whispered love in lightless day.

Years may test, and hope may strain,
But roots grow stronger through the rain.
And I would wait a thousand more,
To find her standing at my shore.

For love is not a race to win,
But a quiet fire that burns within.
And in her arms, the world feels still,
A second chance, a sacred will.

Chapter - XLIV
Chased Stars, Crashed Harder

"The fall spared me, the silence didn't."

It wasn't the fall that tore me apart, it was the silence that shattered my heart.

Chapter – XLIV: Chased Stars, Crashed Harder

Survived The Fall With A Trembling Soul

I chased the stars with burning fire,
Fuelled by faith and pure desire.
I toiled through night and rose through pain,
To touch a sky I'd longed to gain.

I found my place in dreamland's gate,
Where hopes felt full and hands held fate.
Each dawn was golden, pure, and right,
A role that wrapped me in delight.

But even stars can lose their spark,
And fall in silence, cold and dark.
A layoff came like sudden storm,
And broke the bliss I'd just begun to form.

Not just the job, it cracked my core,
My plans, my peace, my dreams of more.
The promises, like glass, were thin,
And shattered loud, but deep within.

I smiled outside, but wept alone,
No hand to hold, no heart to own.
The world moved on, a ruthless cast,
While I stayed lost, tied to the past.

This wouldn't be how stories end,
No path to walk, no will to bend.
And in the hush of one long night,
I lost my breath, and will to fight.

But just before I let go all,
I heard a whisper, faint and small.
Not from a friend, not from the crowd,
But from the sky, both soft and loud.

A chance was sent, a humble start,
To rise again with wiser heart.
To build again from dust and strain,
And walk through storm, not fear the rain.

This time I walk with deeper grace,
With every scar in rightful place.
I'm not just chasing stars above,
I carry galaxies of love.

I'm not the man I was before,
I've opened now a wiser door.
For dreams may fall and roles may die,
But purpose finds another sky.

So if you fall, like I once did,
Don't curse the stars or truths they hid.
For what we lose is not the end,
It's where we break and rebegin.

Chapter - XLV
Spiritual Rebirth

"What died in the dark gave birth to light."

I walked through fire with hands unclean, yet in the ash, His grace was seen. For even the fallen can rise, if they kneel before the skies.

Chapter – XLV: Spiritual Rebirth

Grace After The Grave

I chased the stars with restless feet,
I ran through fire, I drank defeat.
In search of gold, in hunger's flame,
I slowly slipped from heaven's name.

The world grew loud, the soul grew thin,
Desire dressed in holy skin.
I left the altar, left the sky,
For every dream I dared to try.

And when they broke like mirrors thrown,
I faced the truth alone.
No friend could speak the wound I bore,
No voice could calm the inner war.

I sank in silence, deep and blind,
And found how far I'd left behind.
No prayer upon my lips would stay,
No tear could wash the guilt away.

I wasn't pure, I wasn't whole,
I wore the dirt across my soul.
Yet in the dark, I heard Him near,
A whisper soft against my fear.

Not wrath, not fire, not storm, not stone,
But warmth that reached my marrow bone.
He didn't shame, He didn't scorn,
He simply wept for what I'd borne.

I felt His touch within my chest,
Where no one dares to lay or rest.
And though I thought I lost His face,
He found me still, and offered grace.

I said, "I'm stained, I'm not the same,
I've turned far from Your name."
But still He came in dream and lit the flame,
And whispered soft, "I love you, same."

I bowed, I wept, I broke, I knelt,
Not for the sins, but love I felt.
For though I'd fled to chase the wind,
He stood and waited, like a friend.

He is the place I now call home,
The sacred space I used to roam.
And though I walk with wiser eyes,
I walk beneath forgiving skies.

I'm not the child I was before,
But I am His forevermore.
And in my scars, He plants His seed,
To grow the grace my soul will need.

So here I stand, not free from pain,
But drenched in purpose, bathed in rain.
Each step I take, He walks beside,
A Shepherd where my fears still hide.

No longer lost in hunger's fire,
I walk toward His heart's desire.
And every breath, and every birth,
Begins again with spiritual rebirth.

Chapter - XLVI
My Freedom Found Motion

"Each scar became a wing;
I found the strength to spring."

I didn't break free, I fractured with grace, each wound wrote a verse that time couldn't erase."

Chapter – XLVI: My Freedom Found Motion

Sorrow Became My Silent Boon

From broken cries to heights of flame,
I've lived a life that none could name.
I rose from ashes, torn and tossed,
And found myself in what was lost.

Not chasing gold, not chasing fame,
But chasing light beyond the name.
With parents near, with soul unchained,
We drove where only truth remained.

The wheels turned slow, the air turned still,
Through southern winds and ancient hill.
Not for joy or worldly thrill,
But for a silence deep and real.

We reached the lands the clouds called home,
Where rivers sang and spirits roam.
God's country welcomed every breath,
And wrapped my soul in sacred depth.

I prayed not loud, nor asked for more,
I simply knocked on heaven's door.
And in the hush of mountain air,
I found my answers hidden there.

For it was not the temple's stone,
Nor sacred words etched into bone.
Not idols raised or fires that burned,
But love and courage, deeply learned.

The doors I reached were carved divine,
But still, the strength I claimed was mine.
And when I wept without a sound,
His voice in silence wrapped me round.

He said, "My son, through flame and rain,
You rose with strength, endured the pain.
You didn't beg, you didn't hide,
You held your truth and walked with pride."

"The miracles you seek outside,
Have always lived in you, inside.
Stay pure, stay bold, let love be guide,
That's all the armor you'll need to ride."

And so I live, not with regret,
But with a peace I won't forget.
My freedom found its motion true,
Not in escape, but breaking through.

And if you ask where I remain,
It's in the song behind the pain,
In steps I took through storm and stone,
In every truth I called my own.

I am no saint, no perfect man,
Just one who did the best he can.
But if these words still light your night,
Then I have made the journey right.

Chapter - XLVII
A Last Whisper To Mother

"A Whisper Beyond the Womb."

She didn't teach me with words; she taught me with presence. So if I rise and glow, let the world know I am her echo.

Chapter – XLVII: A Last Whisper To Mother

A Thank You For Sacrifice

I searched for words, but none could frame,
The soul behind my silent name.
Each breath I take still holds your grace,
Each tear I hide recalls your face.

I was a child when fate had planned,
A marriage written by unseen hand.
At sixteen years, I wore her grace,
She took me in with heaven's face.

She showed me worlds I'd never seen,
At twenty-one, a soul so keen.
Not just a mother, not just a guide,
She became the ocean I'd confide.

She didn't just bear my name in pride,
She stood through storms and stayed beside.
Through every laugh, through every cry,
Through darkest hours and brightest sky.

She gave me flesh, she gave me bone,
But more than that, she made me home.
She stitched my soul with silent thread,
And walked through fire where angels dread.

She knew my sins, yet chose to stay,
She loved the night inside my day.
She saw the cracks beneath my smile,
And held me close through every trial.

She didn't write the words I weave,
But every line is what she breathed.
She may not grasp the rhymes I sing,
But every verse bears her offering.

She isn't seen in every scene,
But every page has held her sheen.
She lives beneath the ink-stained tide,
The mother who still walks inside.

I owe her more than blood or name,
She is the reason for my flame.
And though one day I fade from view,
My every word will carry you.

You are the dawn I never earned,
The warmth for which my spirit yearned.
And when I'm gone, my books will say,
"She held him up when skies turned gray."

No gold can match her selfless fire,
No fame could rise to lift her higher.
But with this verse, I place her crown,
A queen whose name shall not go down.

She may not read the lines I write,
But every word still holds her light.
One day I'll fade, this frame will fall,
But she will echo through it all.

For ink can do what time denies,
To paint her truth across the skies.
And in these verses, soft and bold,
She'll never age, she'll never glow old.

Immortal now, through voice and verse,
Her love reversed the universe.
She was my heart, my life, my flame,
She gave me soul, she gave me name.

So here, my mother, this I send,
My final thanks from my soul and pen.
For when I pass beyond the shore,
You'll live through me forevermore.

Chapter - XLVIII Bound By Blood Not By Culture

"Tied by blood, but torn by truth."

Bound by veins, but broken by beliefs. The love bloomed in flesh, then lost its place. A sacred bond, lost in culture's chase.

Chapter – XLVIII: Bound By Blood Not By Culture

Love Beyond The Clock Of Time

I met her on one fine winter season,
She was the reason behind my deep poetic emotion.
Our love for each other made our lives sweeter,
Our hearts became each other's shelter.

Every hour we spent together was
adventurous and thrilled,
I am glad that my presence made your life fun-filled.
For hours, we spoke with each other,
I wish those days could have been lasted forever.

Every moment I spent with her was pleasant,
this I can say,
Knowing you are on my side brightens my day.
She was the rhythm of my heart,
And no one can separate us apart.

My poetic lyrics flow out when I see her,
I can't live without her.
Without her I feel out cold,
And she is the woman whom I love the most
in this world.

Our love made our nights sleepless,
Our love for each other is endless.
The feelings we have for each other are priceless,
The shy glance that we hold for each other is matchless.

Our love may smell unmature,
But the fragrance of our feelings is flawlessly pure.
When it comes to feelings, we will never lie,
We will love each other until we die.

My eyes will not close in sleep until I hear her voice,
We loved each other by choice.
There is nothing as noble as her nature,
And I am here with her to love and nurture.

She are my full, bright moon,
And I will be always her own.
We will never depart from each other's eyes,
We will love one another, even after our body dies.

When I look at her, her eyes are on the
ground for a while,
When I looked away, she looked at me with
a timid smile.
The sight of our past caused us pain,
But our love for each other healed us again.

When eye-to-eye answering and eye-to-eye revealing are
there, it's a tale of love,
Where the words of lips are unnecessary to prove.
The single glance of my eye rekindled the life in her,
Even if we are apart, I will always be with her and I will
always be within her.

Each hour with her is a glimpse of splendour,
With hearts unguarded, arms so tender.
The expression of our love is as pleasant as the
moonlight glow,
Our love for each other is a never-ending carnival flow.

I love her lips when they are wet from my kiss,
Only we both know the pleasure of this everlasting bliss.
Her aching heart would yearn to meet me,
She is the only woman who can generate life in me.

I said I would never be parted from her in this life,
She was yearning to be my eternal wife.
Without her, my body and soul suffer altogether,
We want to stay with each other forever.

Without her, I feel so alone,
Just waiting for her to be my own.
I crave her kiss, her soft embrace,
Her lips so near, not one lost space.

Creed was always a barrier on my lover's lip,
I was the only one who made her heart beat skip.
When it comes to feelings, I will never lie,
I will love her until I die.

As darkness waits till lamps grow bright,
I held her close through endless night.
She once said, "You deserve much more,"
But I saw heaven and asked no more.

I knew I was a tender flame,
And every heartbeat called her name.
She faced the world, with storms to weather,
But we chose love, and stayed together.

She feared the weight that love might bear,
Yet in my arms, she found it rare.
No chains to bind, no force, no tether,
Just two hearts choosing forever.

They said we'd part, but still we stood,
Our bond was more than flesh or blood.
And though the world pulled at our thread,
We wove a vow with tears we shed.

We danced through days both bright and grey,
And found new reasons still to stay.
Her voice became my morning song,
Her silence where my soul belongs.

So if you ask what love became,
It wasn't glory, gold, or fame.
It was her eyes, a sacred space,
Where time stood still in love's embrace.

Chapter - XLIX
Miles Without A Map

"Led by pain, saved by grace."

This road won't end; every bruise made me ascend.
Here I write with soul unmasked,
a journey loved and long surpassed.

Chapter – XLIX: Miles Without A Map

In The Silence, I Heard Soul's Direction

I am not a tale that time will close,
Not just a name the silence knows.
I am a story still being penned,
By flesh, by soul, it doesn't end.

I've seen the highs, I've felt the fall,
I've walked through nothing and had it all.
But through it all, through break and bend,
God was always there in the end.

Success came dancing, then slipped away,
Failure came fierce, then learned to pray.
But I remained, not less, not more,
Just truer than I was before.

And now I sit, with pen in hand,
Not to be praised, not to be grand.
But just to write what pain once taught,
That life is breath, and soul is thought.

If tomorrow comes and I am gone,
Know still, my words will carry on.
Not written just with blood or pen,
But with a pulse that beats again and again.

These lines you read, they're not just mine,
They're threads of your own soul in line.
You felt them burn, you felt them bind,
That's how you know we are aligned.

So, if you ever break once more,
And fall again upon the floor,
Reach for these lines, not for my name,
But for the fire that lit your flame.

My words will hold when no one stays,
They'll walk with you through longest days.
Not ink alone, but hope and grace,
A quiet hand in time and place.

This isn't just a writer's page,
It's prayer, it's truth, it's silent rage.
It's love for those who've lost their way,
And still choose light, day after day.

So pass this book with open palm,
To someone stormed, someone without calm.
And let them know they're not alone,
That every heart still finds its home.

And when they ask, "Who wrote this pain?"
Say, "Someone who still speaks in rain".
He may be gone, but hear it clear,
His soul still whispers, 'I am here.'

Because love and kindness never die,
They echo loud beneath the sky.
And that's the tale I choose to send,
A never-ending journey, without end.

Chapter - L
When Breath Becomes Verse

"Where every breath became a line."

Each breath I lost became a line; each scream I hid now speaks in mine. My pain poured out with every verse, a life rewritten verse by verse.

Chapter – L: when breath becomes verse

A Lifetime Carved In Writings

You've walked with me through storm and fire,
Through silent screams and deep desire.
This wasn't ink on pages spread,
But blood I bled, and words I said.

Each line you read was not just mine,
It echoed pain through every spine.
Not just my tale, not just my fall,
But proof that *you* can face it all.

This isn't just a book I wrote,
It's every gasp that filled my throat.
Each chapter wasn't typed with flair,
It came from nights I fought despair.

I wrote of friends who stood like walls,
Of love that bloomed then burned in falls.
Of faith that flickered, rose, and stayed,
God seemed far, but he was never delayed.

I spoke of wounds I kept inside,
Of silent wars I could not hide.
Of shattered truths and stolen peace,
And healing born through slow release.

I don't just call this a memoir from heart,
This is the deepest pulse beneath my heart.
These aren't just stories wrapped in rhyme,
They're beats that kept me stitched through time.

Fifty-five chapters, each a vein,
Pulsing with joy, and holy pain.
And if you've read and felt it true,
Then maybe it's now part of you.

For I believe that stories heal,
When told with truth and not with steel.
And if my voice has made you feel,
Then let your silence, too, reveal.

You, too, have nights that haunt your sleep,
And wounds you bury far too deep.
But if my scars can guide your light,
Then all my pain was worth the fight.

So thank you, friend, for reading me,
For walking through my memory.
This isn't goodbye, nor the final send,
For souls like ours don't truly end.

As long as breath still stirs my chest,
I'll write, I'll bleed, I'll give my best.
For though life flows and time may stray,
My carved-out soul will always stay.

Not a period, but a pen,
I'll write my soul again and then.
Until I fade, or skies descend,
This is my truth. It has no end.

THE END

Author's Note – A Goodbye, Not An End

If you've made it here to the final page, then you've carried pieces of my pain, walked beside my silence, and sat with the shadows I once ran from.

This was not just a book.

It was my blood in ink, my scars in rhyme, and my truth laid bare.

Every poem was carved from a place I never dared to speak aloud. I wept while writing some, trembled through others, and smiled only a little, because not every story is meant to be beautiful.

Some stories are just meant to be told.

You've seen the boy who was almost never born.

You've seen the child whose innocence was stolen.

You've seen the teenager who was mocked, the lover who lost, the man who rose and fell and rose again.

And if even a single moment in these pages reached into your soul and reminded you that **you're not alone**, then my pain has found its purpose and every scar I've shared was worth it.

I don't know who you are.
But I know this:

You've survived something too.
You've held your own "never told" stories.
You've cried silently behind closed doors.
You've loved someone who couldn't love you back.
You've questioned your worth.
And yet, here you are, breathing. Reading. Becoming.

So, if this is goodbye, let it be a brave goodbye.
Goodbye to shame.
Goodbye to silence.
Goodbye to every voice that said you were not enough.

And if we never meet again,
Please promise me one thing:

Tell your story.
Tell it messy. Tell it real.
Even if your voice shakes. Even if your hands bleed.
Because someone, somewhere, aching the way you once did, is waiting for your truth to remind them they still matter, and they are waiting for your truth to save them.

And if you ever forget who you are…
Come back to this book.
We'll remember it together.

- Dr. Prabhakar Shankar

About The Author

Dr. Prabhakar Shankar - A warrior in spirit, a healer in soul, a poet by purpose.

Dr. Prabhakar Shankar is not just a clinical professional. He is a therapist of the human condition. A healer of bodies, a mender of spirits, and a voice for the voiceless, his journey from hardship to hope is nothing short of extraordinary.

His life took a pivotal turn when he was enlightened with technical and management skills under the lights of **IIT Patna**. Within the corridors of one of India's most prestigious institutions, his intellect was sharpened and a deeper purpose awakened. It was here that clinical knowledge met strategic vision, empowering him to lead and shape the evolving world of digital health, where knowledge met clarity, ambition met soul, and vision found its voice.

Born in the margins of silence, shaped by hardship, and raised by resilience, Dr. Prabhakar Shankar turned adversity into his greatest teacher. He rose from the ashes of rejection and silence with one mission to heal through science, through strength, and through story.

He is an internationally acclaimed **gold medallist in martial arts**, a respected **corporate mentor** who has transformed thousands of lives, and a passionate healthcare professional who has stood beside countless patients in their most fragile hours. But his deepest healing power comes through his **pen**.

In his writing, Dr. Prabhakar Shankar does not merely reflect, he reveals. His poetry is raw, unfiltered, and redemptive, pulling truth from trauma and beauty from brokenness. His verses are not written for applause, but for awakening for those fighting unseen wars, carrying invisible grief, and searching for light in quiet corners.

His debut poetic memoir, ***When Breath Becomes Verse***, has been hailed as a literary lifeline, a work that speaks to the human soul, echoing themes of faith, failure, love, resilience, and the sacred act of rising again.

Today, Dr. Prabhakar Shankar leads a life of profound impact, touching patients through digital health, mentoring in boardrooms, and writing from the soul. Whether he's guiding people towards wholeness, shaping young minds with purpose and discipline and soothing silent wounds through verse, one truth remains. His life is his message and every act, a reflection of resilience turned into grace.

He doesn't just treat wounds; he transforms them into wisdom.

A modern-day mystic in a white coat, Dr. Prabhakar Shankar reminds the world that the greatest stories are written not in ink, but in scars, and the strongest voices rise from silence.